T0276405

The 500 Hidden Secrets of
NEW YORK

INTRODUCTION

You've picked up this book, so naturally we assume you've got an inquisitive mind and you don't want to settle for the ordinary. That's why we created this guide, for people like you – the ones who dig deeper, who long to find a true connection to a city's *zeitgeist*.

The suggestions in this book come from a pair of writers who live and thrive on the NYC lifestyle, and can help you weed through an often overwhelming amount of choices. Starting with dining, our streamlined picks are all winners and cover the gamut, from cheap eats to orchestrated tastings. Listed also are off-the-beaten-path museums, memorials, and historic parts of the city that are truly enlightening. When you're ready to stop for a cocktail, coffee, or glass of wine somewhere, we've got you covered with tried-and-true destinations. You'll find out how to enjoy nature within the city – on the water and in the parks – or on a mini-escape. Also included are hot shopping spots, ideas for entertaining nights out, and a handful of hotels that can enhance a stay.
We kept the focus of the book mainly in Manhattan, with some true standouts in the other boroughs. See *Hidden Brooklyn*, our new title, for a more thorough report on that part of town.
The pandemic did a lot to change the energy of some neighborhoods. Downtown remains your best option for nightlife, dining, and shopping. Midtown, though not as jam-packed as it was before Covid, is starting to thrive again.

We hope that our flurry of insider suggestions will help make your experience more personal and memorable, and will inspire you to make your own discoveries.

HOW TO
USE THIS BOOK?

This guide lists 500 things you need to know about New York in 100 different categories. Most of these are places to visit, with practical information like the address and sometimes info on making reservations. Others are bits of information that help you get to know the city and its people. The purpose of this guide is to inspire you to explore the city, but it doesn't cover every aspect from A to Z.

The places in this guide are given an address, including the neighborhood (for example 'Lower East Side' or 'Greenwich Village'), and a number. The neighborhood and number allow you to find the places on the maps at the beginning of the book: first look for the map of the corresponding neighborhood, then look for the right number. A word of caution however: these maps are not detailed enough to allow you to find specific locations in the city. They are included to give you a sense of where places are, and whether they are close by other places of interest. You can obtain an excellent map from any tourist office or in most hotels. Or the addresses can be located on a smartphone.

Please also bear in mind that cities change all the time. The chef who hits a high note one day may be uninspiring on the day you happen to visit. The bar considered one of the 5 most funky bars on the Lower East Side might be empty on the night you're there. This is obviously a highly personal selection. You might not always agree with it. If you want to leave a comment, recommend a bar or reveal your favorite secret place, please visit the website *the500hiddensecrets.com* – you'll also find free tips and the latest news about the series there – or follow *@500hiddensecrets* on Instagram and leave a comment.

THE AUTHORS

Lifelong New York resident **Ellen Swandiak** first became enamored with NYC while attending Parsons School of Design, which inspired a move to a ground-floor apartment in the far West Village. Living in the most colorful and bohemian part of the city taught her to navigate the winding streets of downtown and get to know its many wonderful shops and eateries. In 2005 Ellen moved to a Gramercy high-rise with a winning view of the Empire State Building. Here the idea of a blog was born, now known as *Hobnob Magazine (hobnobmag.com)*, which reports on all her loves: food, drink, style, fun – and parties. As a creative party thrower, Ellen uses ideas inspired by the best chefs and mixologists to include in her fun party themes designed to help people entertain. She can often be spotted, camera in hand, at stylish restaurants and bars, tasting events, and art openings, with her designer eye on the lookout for all that is clever.

Not a day goes by without someone asking Ellen for a tip, but she claims she could not have come up with all these super suggestions without the help of a few friends, so she wishes to thank in particular: Paulina Kajankova who helped name many a fashionable shop, Ronit Schlam, whose knowledge of dance and theater came in handy, and Tom Grant, for letting her run suggestions by him, and who had some great ones of his own.

Katelijne De Backer has called New York City home for over 25 years. Born and raised in Belgium, Katelijne left Brussels for London in 1987, where she spent the next decade. In 1997, New York City called to her and she moved across the pond. As Director of The Armory Show, manager of several other art fairs, and Managing Director of the Lehmann Maupin art gallery, she has worked at the intersection of business and culture her entire career. Katelijne has always had a soft spot for big cities – first Brussels, then London, followed by New York. She moved from Manhattan's Upper West Side to Brooklyn in 2002, and was immediately smitten by her new neighborhood of Brooklyn Heights. Her interest in music, art, food, design, books, and films has taken her to the most fascinating corners of New York City. In 2022 she wrote *Hidden Brooklyn,* where she shares her love of the borough and its unique and lesser-known places with her readers.

NEW YORK

overview

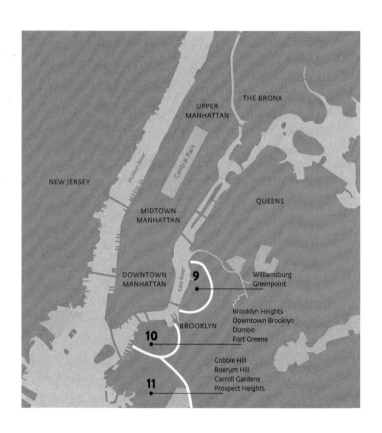

THE BRONX

UPPER
MANHATTAN

NEW JERSEY

Hudson River

Central Park

QUEENS

MIDTOWN
MANHATTAN

DOWNTOWN
MANHATTAN

East River

9 Williamsburg
Greenpoint

Brooklyn Heights
Downtown Brooklyn
BROOKLYN Dumbo
10 Fort Greene

Cobble Hill
Boerum Hill
11 Carroll Gardens
Prospect Heights

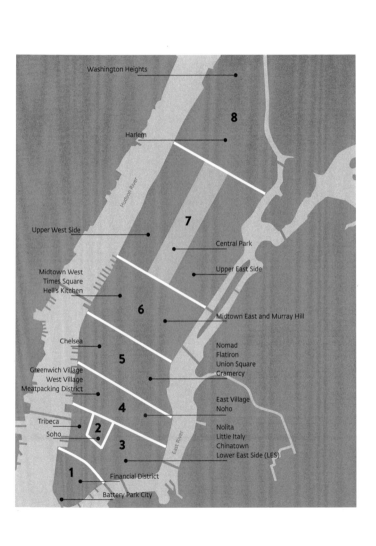

Washington Heights

8

Harlem

Hudson River

Upper West Side

7

Central Park

Midtown West
Times Square
Hell's Kitchen

Upper East Side

6

Midtown East and Murray Hill

Chelsea

5

Nomad
Flatiron
Union Square
Gramercy

Greenwich Village
West Village
Meatpacking District

4

East Village
Noho

Tribeca

2

Soho

3

Nolita
Little Italy
Chinatown
Lower East Side (LES)

East River

1

Financial District

Battery Park City

Map 1

DOWNTOWN MANHATTAN

FINANCIAL DISTRICT
and BATTERY PARK CITY

W Broadway

Broadway

Worth St

299

Chamber St

Warren St

Church St

New York
City Hall

Brooklyn Bridge

Barclay St

297

272

163 277

282

297

Fulton St

440

276

Greenwich St

56

John St

459

116

347

West St

14

Trinity Pl

269

Broadway

Wall St

Water St

32

337

291

Beaver St

FDR Drive

Hudson River

East River

300

267

Pearl St

Battery
Park

336

EAT — **DRINK** — SHOP — BUILDINGS — DISCOVER — **CULTURE** — CHILDREN — SLEEP — WEEKEND

Map 2

DOWNTOWN MANHATTAN

SOHO

Map 3

DOWNTOWN MANHATTAN

TRIBECA, LITTLE ITALY and NOLITA

EAT — **DRINK** — SHOP — BUILDINGS — DISCOVER — **CULTURE** — CHILDREN — SLEEP — WEEKEND

CHINATOWN *and* LOWER EAST SIDE

Map 4

DOWNTOWN MANHATTAN

GREENWICH VILLAGE, WEST VILLAGE and MEATPACKING DISTRICT

EAST VILLAGE *and* NOHO

Map 5

MIDTOWN MANHATTAN

CHELSEA

NOMAD, FLATIRON, UNION SQUARE and GRAMERCY

Map 6

MIDTOWN MANHATTAN

MIDTOWN WEST,
TIMES SQUARE *and* HELL'S KITCHEN

MIDTOWN EAST and MURRAY HILL

Map 7

UPPER WEST SIDE, CENTRAL PARK

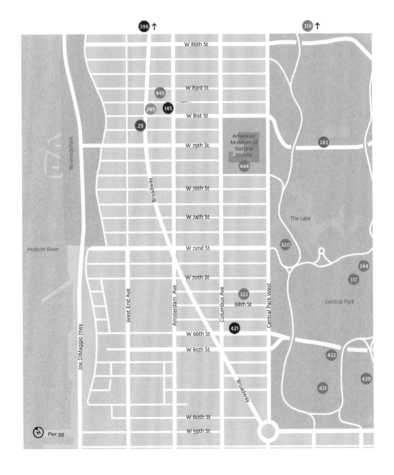

UPPER EAST SIDE

316 ↑

302

394

21

E 85th St

Metropolitan
Museum of Art

386
389
387
390
388

E 83rd St

E 81st St

E 79th St

309

227

203

461

368 162

432

5th Ave

Madison Ave

Park Ave

Lexington Ave

3rd Ave

2nd Ave

1st Ave

York Ave

FDR Drive

E 76th St

E 74th St

432

E 72nd St

377

East River

308

237

E 70th St

99

E 68th St

434

383

E 65th St

435

E 63rd St

138

E 62nd St

E 61st St

462

448

The Pond

E 60th St

340

Ed Koch Queensboro Bridge

339

E 59th St

EAT — DRINK — SHOP — BUILDINGS — DISCOVER — CULTURE — CHILDREN — SLEEP — WEEKEND

Map 8

UPPER MANHATTAN

HARLEM *and* WASHINGTON HEIGHTS

313 304 ↑

THE BRONX

301

331

Harlem

W 155th St

Hudson River

Harlem River Dr

W 145th St

Frederick Douglass Blvd

Adam Clayton Powell Jr Blvd

Malcolm X Blvd / Lenox Ave

W 135th St

Broadway

Amsterdam Ave

5th Ave

Madison Ave

Park Ave

Dr Martin Luther King Jr Blvd

298

287

295

Marcus
Garvey
Park

Lexington Ave

3rd Ave

2nd Ave

1st Ave

248

116th St

Riverside Park

289

Central Park N

110th St

Central Park

Map 9

BROOKLYN

WILLIAMSBURG *and* GREENPOINT

Map 10

BROOKLYN

BROOKLYN HEIGHTS, DOWNTOWN BROOKLYN, DUMBO and FORT GREENE

EAT — **DRINK** — SHOP — BUILDINGS — DISCOVER — **CULTURE** — CHILDREN — SLEEP — WEEKEND

Map 11

BROOKLYN

COBBLE HILL, BOERUM HILL, CARROLL GARDENS *and* PROSPECT HEIGHTS

EAT — **DRINK** — SHOP — BUILDINGS — DISCOVER — **CULTURE** — CHILDREN — SLEEP — WEEKEND

THE BUTCHER'S DAUGTHER

125 PLACES TO EAT OR BUY GOOD FOOD

---

5 places for **BREAKFAST & BREAD** —————— 28

5 friendly places for **BRUNCH** —————— 30

5 interesting places to **DO LUNCH** —————— 32

5 places where **TIME STANDS STILL** —————— 34

5 **CHARMING** restaurants with character —————— 37

5 specialized **FOOD SHOPS** —————— 39

5 **STEAKHOUSES** not Peter Luger's —————— 41

5 authentic places for **BAGELS** —————— 43

The 5 best **HIPSTER** hangouts —————— 45

5 must-try **BURGERS** —————— 48

5 dinners to escape
TIMES SQUARE MADNESS —————— 50

5 **FOOD HALLS** of distinction —————— 52

5 cool **ITALIAN RESTAURANTS** ———————— 54

The 5 best places for **PIZZA** ———————— 56

5 best spots for slurping **OYSTERS** ———————— 58

5 great tastes of **ASIA** ———————— 60

5 spots with extraordinary **TAKE OUT** ———————— 62

5 places with **UNCONVENTIONAL MENUS** —— 64

5 places to satisfy a **SWEET TOOTH** ———————— 66

The 5 best **CONTINENTAL BRASSERIES** ——— 68

5 places to stop at while **GALLERY HOPPING** — 70

5 **VEGETARIAN & VEGAN** *hotspots* ———————— 72

5 faves from a **NEW YORK FOODIE** ———————— 74

5 restaurants for **SEAFOOD** ———————— 76

5 top **TASTING MENUS** ———————— 78

5 places for
BREAKFAST & BREAD

---

1 **LAFAYETTE GRAND CAFÉ & BAKERY**
380 Lafayette St
(at Great Jones St)
East Village ④
+1 212 533 3000
lafayetteny.com

Is it the leather booths, enticing case of pastries, or the belle-époque atmosphere? Never mind why, we love this place. Relax and enjoy artisanal breads, muffins, and assorted pastries baked right on the premises. Or, start your day with one of their fresh-pressed juices to accompany a lively selection of fruit, cereals, eggs, and pancakes.

2 **JACK'S WIFE FREDA**
50 Carmine St
(betw Bleecker and
Bedford St)
Greenwich Village ④
+1 646 669 9888
jackswifefreda.com

An eatery with the sweet ambiance of home. Owned by a husband and wife team – who named the place after their grandparents, who also inspired the menu. Great egg dishes with some Mediterranean flavors thrown in. Rosewater waffles come topped with Lebanese yogurt, mixed berries and honey syrup. Note the cute messages on their sugar packets. There are three more locations in NYC.

3 **BREADS BAKERY**
18 East 16th St
(betw Union Square
W and 5th Ave)
Union Square ⑤
+1 212 633 2253
breadsbakery.com

Here breads come in all shapes and varieties. Challah takes center stage, covered with all sorts of nuts and seeds, among adorable little whole-grain rolls and dense pumpernickel. Pastries, like chocolate rugelach and cookies compete for your attention. Scout out their kiosks on the corner of Bryant park (42nd and 6th Ave) and at Lincoln Center (1890 Broadway).

4 **SULLIVAN STREET BAKERY**
533 West 47th St
Hell's Kitchen ⑥
+1 212 265 5580
*sullivanstreet
bakery.com*

Founded in Soho, where they still have a store at 103 Sullivan Street, this thoroughly Roman bakery is renowned for its outstanding fresh bread, rolls, Roman-style pizzas, and other treats. For over 25 years, their bread has graced the tables of New York's most celebrated restaurants, many of which are mentioned in this book.

5 **THE BUTCHER'S DAUGHTER**
19 Kenmare St
(betw Elizabeth St
and Bowery)
Nolita ③
+1 212 219 3434
*thebutchers
daughter.com*

Ironically named, this spot is a wonderland for vegans and vegetarians. Pop in to get your juice fix, or coconut yogurt parfait, made with ingredients from local farms. They also offer a bunch of egg dishes, plus avocado on toast. There's a second outlet in West Village, on 581 Hudson Street at Bank Street.

5 friendly places for
BRUNCH

6 **ROSEMARY'S**
18 Greenwich Avenue
(at W 10th St)
Greenwich Village ④
+1 212 647 1818
rosemarysnyc.com

The rooftop garden put this place on the map but it's the menu and the ambiance that kept it on the map. There's a long wait sometimes, but enjoying your Italian dish straight from the produce grown on the roof is worth it. In summer French doors open onto the street.

6 ROSEMARY'S

7 BUBBY'S

120 Hudson St
(at N Moore St)
Tribeca ③
+1 212 219 0666
bubbys.com

If you're in for a true American brunch, go to Bubby's. These guys make a point of serving upscale, classic American dishes in a rustic, laidback setting. Try one of their biscuits – a Southern specialty – topped with sausage, jalapeño and eggs, or fried chicken.

8 YUCA BAR

111 Avenue A
(at E 7th St)
East Village ④
+1 212 982 9533
yucabarnyc.com

Hitting brunch here places you squarely in cool environs, perfect for strolling cute shops and people watching. They offer a hearty mix of Latin fusion dishes all under 20 dollars, (add 17 dollars for an hour of bottomless Mimosas or sangria) in a no-frills, funky environment. Warmer weather has tables outside. No reservations.

9 THE SMILE

26 Bond St
(betw Lafayette
and Bowery)
Noho ④
+1 646 329 5836
thesmilenyc.com

This mix of a general store and cafe exudes a rustic, upstate vibe and is a hangout for the young, stylish, arty crowd. Head underground to enjoy the Belgian waffles with caramelized figs. And whatever you order, make sure to get a side of crispy sweet potato hash browns. Fresh muffins, scones, and bread too.

10 UPLAND

345 Park Avenue
South (at 26th St)
Nomad ⑤
+1 212 686 1006
uplandnyc.com

California cuisine is served in a high-ceiling industrial space, with room to breathe. Try the fresh little gem salad, which is so large it's a must-share. There are substantial items like spaghetti topped with fried egg or the Larry David bagel. Creative pizzas and fabulous bottles of wine.

5 interesting places to
DO LUNCH

---

11 LA PECORA BIANCA
1133 Broadway
(at 26th St)
Nomad ⑤
+1 212 498 9696
lapecorabianca.com

La Pecora Bianca is a perfect place to do lunch and sample nicely priced Italian specialties in an airy, industrial whitewashed space. Seasonal and local influence the menu, and even factor into the homemade pastas using whole-wheat and gluten-free grains. The coffee bar transforms into a wine bar later in the day.

12 VESELKA
144 2nd Avenue
(betw St Marks Place
and E 9th St)
East Village ④
+1 212 228 9682
veselka.com

This place is a leftover from when the neighborhood was mostly East European. The menu features *borscht*, beef stroganoff, stuffed cabbage, and a mean Ukrainian keilbasa (smoked pork sausage). Used to be open 24 hours, but has changed to 11 pm weekdays, and 11.30 pm on Friday/Saturday.

13 THE MEATBALL SHOP
798 9th Avenue
(at W 53rd St)
Hell's Kitchen ⑥
+1 212 230 5860
themeatballshop.com

These guys have turned the humble meatball into a superstar. Choose a meat – spicy pork, traditional beef, chicken, or veggie – add a sauce and some sides or get yours on a 'hero' (meaning a big sandwich). A bit packed inside but delicious and no fuss.

14 MANHATTA

28 Liberty St, 60th Fl.
(betw William and
Nassau St)
Financial District ①
+1 212 230 5788
manhatta
restaurant.com

This spot is high in the sky and above it all. In accordance with NYC skyscraper traditions, this place offers extensive, breathtaking views and food that can stop you from looking out the window from one of the city's most beloved restauranteurs. For added fun, head to the rec room with ping-pong table.

15 CRIF DOGS

113 St Marks Place
(betw Ave A
and 1st Ave)
East Village ④
+1 212 614 2728
crifdogs.com

A deep-fried menu of creative hot dogs is the gig here. Dogs come every which way – even a veggie version, and classic NY, which just gets some sauerkraut. Choose from 16 toppings to create your own signature dog, or go for one of their tried-and-true combos like Chihuahua: wrapped in bacon, topped with avodado, sour cream and salsa.

11 LA PECORA BIANCA

5 places where
TIME STANDS STILL

16 **KATZ'S DELICATESSEN**
205 East Houston St
(at Ludlow St)
Lower East Side ③
+1 212 254 2246
katzsdelicatessen.com

New York without Katz's would not be New York. Stick to the classics: the overstuffed corned beef or pastrami sandwiches on rye. While you're there, check out the original World War II sign: 'Send a salami to your boy in the army' and that iconic table where Harry met Sally.

17 **JOHN'S OF 12TH STREET**
302 East 12th St
(betw 1st and 2nd Ave)
East Village ④
+1 212 475 9531
johnsof12thstreet.com

No-frills East Village classic. The place advertises itself as old-school and rightly so. The red sauce that comes with the pasta is the real deal, reminding you either of grandma or of a summer in Italy long ago. Try the chicken Parmigiana. Update: vegan dishes also grace the menu. Cash only.

18 **ZUM STAMMTISCH**
69-46 Myrtle Avenue
(at 70th St)
Glendale, Queens
+1 718 386 3014
zumstammtisch.com

This is of course a German restaurant, where main courses are massive, pork *Schnitzel*, *Sauerbraten*, and all kinds of *Wurst*. The Tyrolean-style place was founded in 1972 by German immigrant John Lehner and is now run by his sons Hans *und* Werner. *Zum Stammtisch* translates to 'at the table for regulars'.

16 KATZ'S DELICATESSEN

19 LA GRENOUILLE

3 East 52nd St
(betw 5th and
Madison Ave)
Midtown East ⑥
+1 212 752 1495
la-grenouille.com

Since 1962 this place has attracted the rich and famous with its sense of tradition and flawless French fare. Known for their towering floral arrangements, white tablecloths, and servers in crisp white jackets, this place is a true slice of New York from a certain era. Now offering late-night jazz, attracting a younger crowd.

20 PIETRO'S

232 East 43rd St
Midtown East ⑥
+1 212 682 9760
pietrosnyc.com

Cozy and curtained and once proclaimed "best steak I ever had" from a famed NYC food critic, Pietro's has been offering the same menu since 1932. The servers are straight out of 1950s Mad Men era and use good old-fashioned personable charm when describing the specials. Come for the chicken parmigiana or a plate of spaghetti and meatballs.

5 CHARMING

restaurants with character

---

21 HÜTTE

1652 2nd Avenue
(betw 85th and
86th St)
Upper East Side ⑦
+1 646 981 0764
huttenyc.com

Located in the outdoor space of Schaller's
Stube, known for its sausage selections,
Hütte is a cool weather concept that
mimics a 1960s alpine ski lodge. From
goulash to spaetzle to fondues, the
journey to the alps is complete, including
the cold temperature. When the weather
warms up, Hütte becomes Blume, and
blooms into a garden oasis with pink
chairs and Austrian wines.

22 BROOKLYN DINER

212 West 57th St
(betw 7th Ave
and Broadway)
Midtown East ⑥
+1 212 977 1957
brooklyndiner.com

This nostalgic diner is around the
corner from Carnegie Hall and close
to Central Park. It's outfitted in plush
brown leather stools and banquettes, and
booths adorned with brass nameplates of
celebrity patrons. Go for the cheeseburger
with fried battered onions on top, or their
popular chicken potpie, or a milkshake.

23 TEA & SYMPATHY

108 Greenwich Avenue (betw Horatio and Jane St)
Greenwich Village ④
+1 212 989 9735
teaandsympathy.com

One of the nicest things about NYC is the ability to experience other cultures without leaving town. This place is a haven for those craving British comfort food like bangers and mash, Welsh rarebit, black pudding – and of course a proper cup of tea served in charming traditional mismatched china with fresh scones and clotted cream and tea sandwiches.

24 MOLLY'S

287 3rd Avenue (betw E 22nd and 23rd St)
Gramercy ⑤
+1 212 889 3361
mollysshebeennyc.com

Molly's is a true Irish *shebeen* with sawdust on the floor and multiple Guinness taps manned by skilled pourers. The menu offers fantastic versions of Irish favorites like shepherd's pie along with exceptional American bar faves. This place is an especially welcome spot in winter, with a fireplace to take the chill away.

25 LE COUCOU

138 Lafayette St (at Howard St)
Soho ②
+1 212 271 4252
lecoucou.com

Refined and French and the talk-of-the-town inside the New York French community. With a wink to long-gone Manhattan institution Lutece, Chef Daniel Rose (of La Bourse et La Vie in Paris) goes back to the cuisine's roots. Enjoy your meal in an exquisitely proportioned and well-designed space, with just the right touch of rusticity.

5 specialized
FOOD SHOPS

26 **EAST VILLAGE MEAT MARKET / J. BACZYNSKY**
139 2nd Avenue
(betw 8th and 9th St)
East Village ④
+1 212 228 5590
eastvillage
meatmarket.com

One of the city's favorite butcher shops with an enduring history, this market is a treasure in what is known as Little Ukraine. Expect high quality and reasonable prices. Go back in time with their old-fashioned *kielbasa* creations and attentive service. If you find yourself in New York during October, join them in celebrating Pierogi day.

27 **DI PALO'S FINE FOODS**
200 Grand St
(betw Mott and Mulberry St)
Little Italy ③
+1 212 226 1033

A 100-year-old market with outrageously good Italian specialities. So good, there is usually a line that wraps around the corner. It's take-out only, so get some goodies to-go and have yourself a picnic. Tasting helps you decide. Go for the fresh mozzarella and the fresh porchetta.

28 **DÉPANNEUR**
242 Wythe Avenue
(at N 3rd St)
Williamsburg, Brooklyn ⑨
+1 347 227 8424
depanneur.com

Here's a great stop in Williamsburg: a market, deli, and coffee shop in one. The grocery items are upscale – how could it be otherwise with such a delicious name. Sandwiches here are creative – like the proscuitto, fig jam and fresh mozzarella.

29 ZABAR'S

2245 Broadway
(at W 80th St)
Upper West Side ⑦
+1 212 787 2000
zabars.com

The Sunday morning ritual for many upper west siders. This 'temple of fish' was founded by Louis and Lilian Zabar in 1934 and is still going strong three generations later. Be seduced by all kinds and often hard to find smoked fish, caviar, dried fruit, cheeses, meats, and olives, all of the best quality.

30 MURRAY'S CHEESE

254 Bleecker St
(betw 6th and 7th St)
Greenwich Village ④
+1 212 243 3289
murrayscheese.com

A NYC legend on Bleecker Street has expanded into a mega foodie playground. In addition to offering a mind-boggling selection of cheeses, they've got a market loaded with packaged goods, a bulging charcuterie section, and a take-out area featuring decadent grilled cheese sandwiches. There's space upstairs for eating or attending a class.

29 ZABAR'S

5 STEAKHOUSES
not Peter Luger's

31 **KEENS STEAKHOUSE**
72 West 36th St
(at 6th Ave)
Midtown ⑥
+1 212 947 3636
keens.com

Opened in 1885, this steakhouse takes you back in time with its patrons' 90.000 clay pipes, numbered and mounted on the ceiling. The mutton chop is popular, but all the cuts of meat are extraordinary. Be prepared for enormous portions. A clubby, Victorian vibe in the bar accompanies its extensive single malt selection.

32 **DELMONICO'S**
56 Beaver St
(at S William St)
Financial District ①
+1 212 509 1144
delmonicos.com

Fancy? Yes, luxurious even. Housed in a stunning triangular building way downtown, the Delmonico brothers opened this place in 1837. Known for the large wine cellar and as the birthplace of the Delmonico steak, a juicy cut of rib eye served with a single onion ring on top.

33 **OLD HOMESTEAD**
56 9th Avenue
(betw 14th and 15th St)
Meatpacking
District ④
+1 212 242 9040
*theoldhomestead
steakhouse.com*

Located on the edge of the Meatpacking District, this place existed when the area actually was a center of meat distribution for the city, in 1868. Marked by the iconic lifesize cow that sits atop the entrance. Be prepared to spend – on colossal crab cakes, and signature prime rib – as you dine with fellow VIPs.

34 AMERICAN CUT

363 Greenwich St
(betw Franklin
and Harrison St)
Tribeca ③
+1 212 226 4736
*americancut
steakhouse.com*

For something a little more of this century, check out Chef Marc Forgione's take on the steakhouse. He pioneered a pastrami spice rub to flavor his rib eye. Top your steak with one of five sauces or farm fresh egg or bone marrow. Raw bar includes his signature chili lobster. Two locations in Manhattan.

35 STRIP HOUSE

13 East 12th St
(betw University Pl
and 5th Ave)
Greenwich Village ④
+1 212 328 0000
striphouse.com

Alluding to the name, red leather banquettes, photos of pin ups and dim lighting set the scene in this underground lair. In addition to classic steaks like the New York Strip, they offer a full raw bar, and the usual sides with a little more: goose-fat potatoes and black truffle creamed spinach, are taste sensations.

32 DELMONICO'S

5 authentic places for
BAGELS

36 **MURRAY'S BAGELS**
500 6th Avenue
(betw 12th and 13th St)
Greenwich Village ④
+1 212 462 2830
murraysbagels.com

Nothing is more New York than bagels, and this one is our favorite. Until recently Murray's refused to toast their bagels, so convinced they were about their outstanding fare. Get the egg sandwich or any bagel with lox and cream cheese and enjoy on the bench outside.

37 **TOMPKINS SQUARE BAGELS**
165 Avenue A
(at E 10th St)
East Village ④
+1 646 351 6520
tompkinssquare
bagels.com

Bagels done the traditional way: rolled by hand, then boiled before baking. Twenty seven cream cheese flavors accompany the bagels, including the surprising, pastel-colored Birthday Cake, delightful for kids. As for bagel varieties, they also carry five types of gluten-free bagels and a spelt bagel. Long lines on weekends. So popular, they opened two more locations.

38 **BAGEL HOLE**
400 7th Avenue
(betw 12th and 13th St)
Park Slope,
Brooklyn ⑪
+1 718 788 4014
bagelhole.net

Mayor Bill de Blasio, calls it 'The bagel you would have gotten a century ago'. Their winning formula uses malt instead of sugar, and can be enjoyed with or without cream cheese (or 'schmear' in proper New York lingo).

39 BLACK SEED BAGELS

176 1st Avenue
(at E 11th St)
East Village ④
+1 646 859 2289
blackseedbagels.com

Montreal's interpretation of the bagel. Slightly smaller, these are hand rolled, boiled in honey water, then baked in a wood-fired oven. Old-style mosaics and geometric wood benches make up the scene. Creative sandwiches in addition to the usual. Try the pretty pink Tobiko cream cheese with smoked salmon. Other locations: Nolita, Fidi, Nomad, Brooklyn Heights.

40 ZUCKER'S BAGELS & SMOKED FISH

146 Chambers St
(betw W Broadway
and Greenwich St)
Tribeca ③
+1 212 608 5844
zuckersbagels.com

Owner Matt Pomerantz grew up eating in all the Jewish restaurants that once graced the neighborhood, and left his job on Wall Street to run Zucker's. They keep it real in an ever more gentrifying Tribeca with 13 types of smoked and pickled fish, 9 cream cheeses, and 16 styles of bagels.

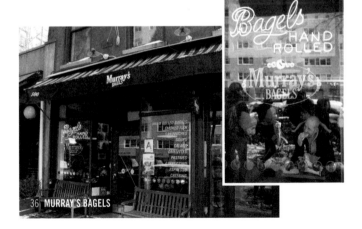

36 MURRAY'S BAGELS

The 5 best
HIPSTER
hangouts

41 **SONS OF ESSEX**
   133 Essex St
   (betw Rivington
   and Stanton St)
   Lower East Side ③
   +1 212 674 7100
   sonsofessexnyc.com

Basically a night club with food, or
a clubby restaurant if you will, where
folks arrive dressed up and ready to party.
Though quite good, the food is not the
object here, the party atmosphere is.
Go behind the deli storefront to enter
a bustling bar scene in an eclectic setting
with DJ and occasional celebrity drop-ins.

42 **DINER**
   85 Broadway
   (at Berry St)
   Williamsburg,
   Brooklyn ⑨
   +1 718 486 3077
   dinernyc.com

Cool is key here even though it has been
around for a while, the neighborhood
(southern stretch of Williamsburg) has
changed and it has been noted that more
visitors – foreign and not – frequent this
place than before. Set in a narrow metal
dining car from the twenties. Creative,
hand-done menus.

43 THE WREN

**344 Bowery
(betw Bond and
3rd St)
East Village** ④
+1 212 388 0148
thewrennyc.com

Six blocks from Washington Square Park and close to the Bowery Hotel, this East Village hang out on the Bowery feels like a studied English farmhouse, but with a hipster ambiance. Of course, you can order your fish and chips and fried calamari, but since they are known more for their cocktails, focus on these.

44 MISS LILY'S

**132 West Houston St
(at Sullivan St)
Soho** ②
+1 646 588 5375
misslilys.com

A cool Caribbean hangout that has its own radio station on the premises, so you can get your reggae fix while chowing down. Snack on the jerk corn topped with mayo and toasted coconut, hot pepper shrimp, or grilled branzino in scotch bonnet brown butter. Photos of Grace Jones grace the walls for your viewing pleasure.

45 FREEMANS

**End of Freeman Alley
(off Rivington St
betw Chrystie St
and Bowery)
Lower East Side** ③
+1 212 420 0012
freemansrestaurant.com

Hidden in an alley off Rivington Street a dual level of small rooms create the feel of a clandestine colonial American tavern exemplified by its rugged decor, creaky wooden floors, and a glut of taxidermy. The menu is all American as well. Try the whole grilled trout, served with thyme, garlic oil and lemon.

45 FREEMANS

5 must-try
BURGERS

46 **SHAKE SHACK**

**Madison Square Park
(SE corner off 23rd St)
Flatiron** ⑤
+1 212 889 6600
shakeshack.com

The original mothership of Danny Meyer's global chain has served its much desired burger – an upscale rendition of its fast-food cousins – here since 2004. Stand in line and order all the toppings. Or download the official Shake Shack app to order ahead and choose a pick-up time.

47 **THE SPANIARD**

**190 West 4th St
(at Barrow St)
Greenwich Village** ④
+1 212 918 1986
thespaniardnyc.com

Great spot to meet attractive people, slink into a leather banquette, and indulge in upscale pub food. They're known for their extensive whiskey selection and the Smash Burger, which consists of a double order of smashed patties, cooked crispy and topped with American cheese, lettuce, and pickles.

48 **4 CHARLES PRIME RIB**

**4 Charles St
(betw Greenwich Ave
and Waverly Pl)
West Village** ④
nycprimerib.com

Within the ambiance of a proper steakhouse – heavily paneled walls with leather banquettes and vintage prints – you will feast on the burger made famous in Chicago, a double patty covered in American cheese served with pickles, mayo and Dijon. This is a place for late-night indulgence.

49 BURGER JOINT
AT: THOMPSON CENTRAL
PARK HOTEL
**119 West 56th St
Midtown West ⑥
+1 212 708 7414**
burgerjointny.com

This dive-y burger joint has been sitting off the lobby of a fancy hotel since 2002. Recently reopened in its glorious unglamorous, bare bones atmosphere, Burger Joint serves their fast-food style patties with The Works: lettuce, tomato, onion, sliced pickles, mustard, ketchup, and mayo. Make sure to add your name to the graffitied wall for posterity.

50 VIA CAROTA
**51 Grove St
(betw Bleecker
and W 4th St)
West Village ④
+1 212 255 1962**
viacarota.com

This seasonally driven Italian restaurant offers a most unusual burger, known as the hand-chopped grass-fed steak. Served sans bun, it is charred on two sides and red in the middle. Strictly for meat loving purists. They've filled the space with antique china and other charming touches, from the team of chefs that own Buvette and I Sodi.

46 SHAKE SHACK

5 dinners to escape
TIMES SQUARE MADNESS

---

51 VALERIE

45 West 45th St
(betw 5th and 6th Ave)
Midtown West ⑥
+1 212 302 4545
valerienewyorkcity.com

Last time I went to the theater this place was one of the few serving dinner till 11.30 pm. The reward for the short hike to get there was their juicy signature burger and modern Waldorf salad. It's a welcome oversized space with glamorous bar, for those looking for a late-night cocktail and room to spread out.

52 THE LAMBS CLUB

132 West 44th St
(betw 6th Ave and
Broadway)
Times Square ⑥
+1 212 997 5262
thelambsclub.com

This place is class personified. Unwind in their plush red banquettes while sipping a stellar glass of wine or cocktail. Chef Zakarian's dishes never fail to please. If you get there early, there's usually a lively jazz trio filling the space with cool sounds. Book the bar downstairs if you are just doing drinks and bar snacks.

53 THE BLUE DOG

308 West 50th St
(betw 8th and 9th Ave)
Times Square ⑥
+1 212 459 0700
bluedognyc.com

Blue Dog is a surprisingly cozy cafe out of the fray of the Times Square crowds. Vintage movies are projected on the wall, and they have a great soundtrack playing. The menu is straightforward and leans to the healthy end of the spectrum with lots of salads, burgers, fish, and some pastas to please all palates. Brunch and lunch too.

54 GLASS HOUSE TAVERN

252 West 47th St
(betw Broadway
and 8th Ave)
Times Square ⑥
+1 212 730 4800
glasshousetavern.com

A down-to-earth find amidst the clamor of Times Square. The menu features classic fare: meats, fish, some pastas/risotto, and salads, with a prix fixe that's a deal. Dinner is served till midnight, the bar is open till 1 am (pre Covid this was an even later haunt). Broadway actors are known to frequent here after a show.

55 SEN SAKANA

28 West 44th St
(betw 5th and 6th Ave)
Midtown West ⑥
+1 212 221 9560
sensakana.com

This place is just east of the heart of Times Square, on a block that had no less than seven hotspots during pre-Covid days. My number one choice for pre theater is Sen Sakana, to feast on some of the most delicious ceviches and creative sushi rolls at this Japanese Peruvian spot. Hot apps: the beef skewers and the dumplings are fab.

5 FOOD HALLS
of distinction

---

56 LE DISTRICT
AT: BROOKFIELD PLACE
225 Liberty St
(on the Hudson River)
Battery Park City ①
+1 212 981 8588
ledistrict.com

Right near the 9/11 Memorial is a mecca for all that is French. Peruse mustards, breads, cheese, *pâté*, even a chocolate mousse bar. Restaurants on the scene include: Beaubourg serving proper French classics; L'Appart the Michelin-rated intimate 28-seat boîte; at Le Bar toast a cocktail with Wall Street workers.

57 MOTT STREET EATERY
98 Mott St
(betw Canal and
Hester St)
Chinatown ③
@mott.street.eatery

Once housing Joy Luck Palace, a famous dim sum hall, this is now a 10-stall food hall focused on Chinatown's various cuisines. 89 Eatery offers its version of dim sum and uncommonly crispy skin pipa duck. Other spots offer bubble tea, unusual and rare sushi, specialty teas, and even Asian pizza.

58 URBANSPACE VANDERBILT
Vanderbilt Avenue
(at E 45th St)
Midtown East ⑥
+1 646 747 0810
urbanspacenyc.com

This is a great spot to get a taste of many of NYC's famed restaurants, all in one spot. Try tacos from La Palapa, pizza from Roberta's, fried chicken from Delaney Chicken, and finish with a sweet from Ovenly, camping out at one of their communal picnic tables. Right across from Grand Central.

59 DEKALB MARKET HALL
445 Albee Sq West
(betw Willoughby
and Fulton St)
Downtown
Brooklyn ⑩
+1 929 359 6555
dekalbmarkethall.com

Brooklyn's largest food hall features classic tastes of New York (think Katz) and newfangled bites covering all foodie leanings. If you've worked up an appetite having crossed the Brooklyn Bridge and explored the Downtown Brooklyn sites, like the Transit Museum or Barclays Center, this place will provide provisions from 11 am to 9 pm.

60 CHELSEA MARKET
75 9th Avenue
(betw 15th and 16th St)
Chelsea ⑤
+1 212 652 2121
chelseamarket.com

Located near the High Line, this place is a foodie mecca. Stock up on culinary gifts in Chelsea Market Baskets, or decorative imports from Marrakesh and Pearl River Mart. Hungry? Cappone's makes 30 different sandwiches featuring salumi on freshly baked bread, try the battered fish tacos from Los Mariscos, or ice cream at L'Arte del Gelato, just to name a few.

56 LE DISCTRICT

5 cool
ITALIAN RESTAURANTS

---

61 **SUPREMA PROVISIONS**
305 Bleecker St (betw Grove and Barrow St)
Greenwich Village ④
+1 646 964 4994
supremanyc.com

This place is a market/restaurant, so after your meal you can stock up on Italian goodies to go. Go for the exceptional charcuterie here with a glass of wine, or one of their fresh pastas. The ambiance feels like an adorable, old-fashioned mart with rustic wooden stools and marble tables. Bonus: the burger with ample melted cheese and black garlic sauce.

62 **MORSO**
420 East 59th St (betw 1st Ave and Sutton Pl)
Midtown East ⑥
+1 212 759 2706
morso-nyc.com

This place is the real deal – it feels almost like actually being in Italy. Most of the ingredients come directly from there, including the famous chef, who fawns over guests in the most loving and welcoming way. Morso means 'bite' so you can sample the gamut here. During warmer months the outside garden is divine.

63 GNOCCO

337 East 10th St
(betw Ave A and B)
East Village ④
+1 212 677 1913
gnocco.com

Simple Italian fare, located across from Tompkins Square Park. Named for the fried dough puffs that you get with prosciutto and salami in Modena, is also its excellent namesake dish. Fifteen styles of pizzas are great for sharing. Ideally located off Ave B's line up of bars, with the most appealing backyard patio in summer.

64 EMILIO'S BALLATO

55 East Houston St
(betw Mulberry
and Mott)
Nolita ③
+1 212 274 8881
ballatos.com

Faded artistic walls with haphazardly strewn photos of former clientele welcome you to Godfather-style Italian. Known for attracting celebrities (including a recent visit by Barack Obama and his daughter) it's also known for owner Emilio Vitolo, a man with personality, who likes to interact with guests. The menu is pure southern Italian, so get the meatballs.

65 LILIA

567 Union Avenue
(at N 10th St)
Williamsburg,
Brooklyn ⑨
+1 718 576 3095
lilianewyork.com

Missy Robbins, known for her pasta and original sauces, is at the helm of this former auto-body shop that's been transformed into a gray-and-beige retreat. Try her squash-filled ravioli with hazelnuts and sage or the more daring spaghetti with anchovies and caramelized onions – you will not want the meal to end. The adjoining cafe serves coffee, switches to sandwiches and gelato, then a cocktail bar at 5 pm.

The 5 best places for
PIZZA

---

66 BLEECKER STREET PIZZA
69 7th Avenue South
(at Bleecker St)
Greenwich Village ④
+1 212 924 4466
bleeckerstreetpizza.com

The hole-in-the-wall atmosphere should not deter you from sampling pizza here. The plain cheese slice with perfectly marbled mozzarella and sauce is a New York archetype. Another favorite: the Nonna Maria with homemade marinara, fresh mozzarella and basil. Open till 5 am Friday thru Sunday. They also offer wine and beer.

67 JULIANA'S
19 Old Fulton St
(betw Water
and Front St)
Dumbo, Brooklyn ⑲
+1 718 596 6700
julianaspizza.com

Home of the original, hand-built, blazingly hot coal oven, Juliana's is the come-back-to-life Grimaldi's, one of NY's most famous pizza places. Deliciously crispy and airy thin crusts still reign here, adorned with nice homemade toppings. Grimaldi's, around the corner, and Juliana's are locked in a stiff competition, so go and try both to see for yourself.

68 ROBERTA'S

261 Moore St
(betw White
and Bogart St)
Bushwick,
Brooklyn ⑨
+1 718 417 1118
robertaspizza.com

Accompanied by rock music from their
in-house radio station you can enjoy
a pizza that's become a global brand.
One of the earliest pioneers in Bushwick,
they've set up picnic tables, and a tiki
bar behind grafitti'd cinder block facade.
Try the Famous Original with tomato,
mozzarella, caciocavallo, and parmigiano
cheeses, with oregano and chili. Less
mobbed at lunch.

69 EMMY SQUARED

364 Grand St
(at S 1st St)
Williamsburg,
Brooklyn ⑨
+1 718 360 4535
*emmysquared
pizza.com*

Detroit-style-pizza is served here, which
means a soft, crunchy, not-too-thick crust,
with cheese baked right into it. A beloved
cilantro mint ranch dressing from their
debut restaurant Emily's comes into play
here on the signature pie, the Emmy,
with mozzarella, banana peppers, slivered
onions and a bowl of tangy marinara
for dipping.

70 PAULIE GEE'S

60 Greenpoint Ave
(betw West and
Franklin St)
Greenpoint,
Brooklyn ⑨
+1 347 987 3747
pauliegee.com

Reading the Paulie Gee menu is a joy in
itself – a sampling of the pizza names:
Ricotta Be Kiddin' Me, Feel Like Bacon
Love, Anise and Anephew, and Simply
Red. The part-warehouse, part-farmhouse
space boasts rustic wooden tables with
a huge tiled-brick oven imported from
Italy. Many vegetarian/vegan options
grace the menu.

5 best spots for slurping
OYSTERS

---

71 **TERROIR TRIBECA**
   24 Harrison St
   (betw Greenwich
   and Hudson St)
   Tribeca ③
   +1 212 625 9463
   wineisterroir.com

At Terroir, you can not only indulge on three oyster varieties and snacks like popcorn and boquerones (with Happy Hour pricing), but you can treat yourself to a lovingly curated wine list by the inimitable Paul Grieco to pair them with. Communal high top tables encourage mingling, while exposed brick walls lend a relaxed vibe.

72 **LAZY POINT**
   310 Spring St
   (betw Hudson
   and Greenwich St)
   Tribeca ③
   lazypointnyc.com

An out-of-the-way spot that's styled as if beach-side with cheerful nautical motifs. It's also great for cocktails and late-night dancing. This block hosts a few other hot spots, but this place is unassuming. On the menu: Montauk Pearls in mignonette or Lazy Point Bloody Mary Oysters.

73 **JEFFREY'S GROCERY**
   172 Waverly Place
   (at Christopher St)
   West Village ④
   jeffreysgrocery.com

An unassuming underdog in the raw seafood category, this spot could be easily overlooked when walking by. But their oyster and other raw bar and seafood offerings shine. Share the Le Jeffrey seafood tower, which includes smoked mussels, lobster salad and tuna conserva.

74 MERMAID OYSTER BAR

89 MacDougal St
(betw Bleecker and
W Houston St)
West Village ④
+1 212 260 0100
themermaidnyc.com

Devoted to a menu of food from the sea, this buzzing, monotone spot is staged simply with walls of photos. They take oyster-ing seriously and offer seven to eight varieties to choose from on the daily roster. Happy hour every day from 4.30 to 6.30 pm with 1,25-dollar oysters. They also have locations in Chelsea and Upper West Side.

75 CULL & PISTOL

AT: CHELSEA MARKET

75 9th Avenue
(betw 9th and
10th Ave)
Chelsea ⑤
+1 646 568 1223
cullandpistol.com

Whether you have been gallery hopping or wandering Meatpacking, stop in for an oyster fix. An assortment of twelve oyster varieties dominate the raw bar menu, with half-priced oysters happening Monday through Friday from 4 pm to 6 pm. Try the Oysters Kilpatrick which are grilled with garlic butter, bacon, pickled shallot and sautéed kale.

5 great tastes of
ASIA

---

76 RED FARM

**529 Hudson St
(betw Charles
and W 10th St)
West Village** ④
+1 212 792 9700
redfarmnyc.com

A restaurant that delivers playful and
artistic renditions of Chinese fare with
a farm-to-table sensibility. Think pastel-
colored Pac Man shrimp dumplings,
sculptural chicken salad, and pastrami
egg rolls. Gluten-free-ers may also delight
in their assortment of noodles, dim sum
and dumplings, served with GF soy sauce.
There's a second location on the UWS.

77 TIM HO WAN USA

**85 4th Avenue
(at 10th St)
East Village** ④
+1 212 228 2800
timhowanusa.com

This famed Hong Kong-based chain has
finally made it to America onto this
New York corner. Specializing in dim
sum served day and night. You can eat
sitting down or standing up at the bar in
a minimally decorated room. A busy place
that took off since its opening in 2016.

78 BOHEMIAN

57 Great Jones St
(betw Bowery and
Lafayette St)
Noho ④
*playearth.jp/
bohemian_ny*

For those who love a challenge, this place only accepts guests who have been introduced by previous diners. The spot is located in a historical building whose interiors hosted Andy Warhol and Jean-Michel Basquiat. If you do not have a referral you can email them and make your case. The reward is a roster of bar snacks, sashimi and pricey, specialty cuts of Wagyu beef.

79 CHOP-SHOP

254 10th Avenue
(betw 24th and
25th St)
Chelsea ⑤
+1 212 820 0333
chop-shop.co

Get a dose of classic pan-Asian dishes done to perfection. Small bites include assorted summer rolls, lamb or vegetable dumplings, and rack of ribs. Noodles and rice dishes also factor in. The space has a zen, industrial feel with whitewashed brick walls, and pine stools. Backyard dining during warmer months.

80 YAMA

122 East 17th St
(at Irving Place)
Union Square ⑤
+1 212 475 0969
yamanyc.com

This slightly underground spot, in the building once a home to Washington Irving, is on a quaint corner a block from Union Square Park. Since 1988, they have been wowing those in the know with their nicely priced, creative sushi and Japanese specialties. No reservations, so there may be a wait.

5 spots with extraordinary
TAKE OUT

---

81 **BRODO**
200 1st Avenue
(at E 12th St)
East Village ④
+1 646 602 1300
brodo.com

The take out window attached to upscale Hearth restaurant offers a 'hot' new concept. They offer only sipping broths and soups at Brodo (Italian for broth) in celebration of broth's inherent curative qualities. Broth is served in cups for you to sip as you would a coffee. Locations are popping up everywhere.

82 LA ESQUINA

82 LA ESQUINA

114 Kenmare St
(at Lafayette St)
Nolita ③
+1 646 613 7100
esquinanyc.com

Market-fresh Mexican food from a spot that every downtown New Yorker recognizes: the cool triangle building along Kenmare where food can be had from: the taqueria (sliced rib eye), the brasserie (*costillas de res* – slow roasted beef short ribs) and the cafe (*los waffles*).

83 CAFÉ HABANA

17 Prince St
(at Elizabeth St)
Nolita ③
+1 212 625 2001
cafehabana.com

This very popular, tight Cuban eatery is known for their delectable Mexican grilled corn or their Habana Cuban sandwich – a citrus-marinated roast pork, with Swiss cheese, chipotle mayonnaise, and pickle. Next door, the Habana-To-Go has the same menu, packed to go.

84 DORADO TACOS

28 East 12th St
(betw University Pl
and 5th Ave)
Greenwich Village ④
+1 212 627 0900
doradotacos.com

A counter service Mexican eatery specializing in Baja-style fish tacos in a tiny space overlooking the New York University student hustle and bustle on University Place. Tacos also come with steak, chicken, shrimp, chorizo, and vegetarian choices. Wash it all down with a Mexican beer, to stay authentic.

85 'WICHCRAFT

1407 Broadway
(betw 38th and
39th St)
Midtown West ⑥
+1 646 329 6025
wichcraft.com

Celebrity chef Tom Collichio's take on the sandwich. Breakfast sandwiches are available throughout the day for those hankering a melty egg 'n' cheese. Pressed paninis oozing with Gruyère and Cuban-style pork or kale compete with more healthful combinations, like tuna with fennel and tapenade, for your attention.

5 places with
UNCONVENTIONAL MENUS

---

86 **KING**

18 King St
(at 6th Ave)
Greenwich Village ④
+1 917 825 1618
kingrestaurant.nyc

This minimalist spot off the beaten track offers intimate digs to enjoy an ever-changing menu of surprise ingredients. Do order their staple, panisse, chickpea flour which resemble bread sticks, but are altogether different – hot and salty with fried sage leaves. Main dishes could be as exotic as bollito misto of ox-tongue and cotechino with lentils, fresh horseradish cream and dragoncello.

87 **ESTELA**

47 East Houston St,
1st Fl.
(betw Mott and
Mulberry St)
Soho ③
+1 212 219 7693
estelanyc.com

One flight up takes you to a rustic, high-ceiling room with large marble bar and raucous New York spirit. Each dish has an unusual twist or off-the-wall ingredient that will excite and keep any foodie on their toes. Examples are the grilled foie gras and grape leaf or beef tartare with elderberries and sunchoke that arrive as small plates that you can share.

88 SHUKO

47 East 12th St
(betw Broadway and
University Pl)
Greenwich Village ④
+1 212 228 6088
shukonyc.com

Owners Nick and Jimmy both worked at legendary Masa, and have developed one of the city's best sushi tasting menus, with menu items based on what looks freshest that day, combined with exotic ingredients from far-away locales. Forgoing tradition, some of their combinations can be a little on the edge. Also known for their artisanal sakes, and cocktails.

89 GEM

116 Forsyth St
(betw Broome and
Delancey St)
Lower East Side ③
+1 917 741 8954
gem-nyc.com

Chef Flynn McGarry started serving tasting menus at the age of 19 to much acclaim. His casual approach to high-end dishes with interesting combinations is the draw. Some veggie-centric a la carte dishes: smoked mussels with artichokes and green olives; beets and strawberries in smoked tea broth with vadouvan oil; grilled lobster with smoked chili, cucumber leaves and burnt bay leaf oil.

90 MOKYO

109 St Marks Place
(betw Ave A and
1st Ave)
East Village ④
+1 646 850 0650
mokyony.com

Chef Kyungmin Kay Hyun's artistry comes from having worked in the kitchens of ABC Kitchen and Jean-Georges, her Korean background and her travels to Peru and Spain. Her lovingly styled tapas reflect these elements in a single dish, all at affordable prices. Try the Corn Dumplings served with truffle salsa verde, fennel, and parmigiano.

5 *places to satisfy a*
SWEET TOOTH

---

91 AMPLE HILLS CREAMERY

141 8th Avenue
(betw 16th and 17th St)
Chelsea ⑤
+1 646 454 0440
amplehills.com

Brooklyn's favorite ice-cream shop now has spots dotted around Manhattan and Queens. Made with hormone-free cream from grass-fed cows. Flavors are whimsical, irresistible mixes. The Ooey Gooey Butter Cake adds hunks of St Louis-style cake to its vanilla. For sweet/savory lovers, the Munchies throws a realm of snacks into its signature pretzel-infused ice cream – crackers, potato chips and mini M&M's.

92 CHIKALICIOUS DESSERT BAR

203 East 10th St
(betw 1st and 2nd Ave)
East Village ④
+1 212 995 9511
thedessertclub.com

From a famed pastry chef Chika Tillman comes an assortment of sweets that can make your head spin. Choose from the Dough'ssant – a mix between a doughnut and croissant, covered in various flavors – cupcakes, breads, cookies, macarons, and layer cakes. If you can't decide, just order the dessert Omakase, chosen by the chef.

93 RING DING BAR

**179 Duane St
(betw Greenwich
and Hudson St)
Tribeca ③**
ringdingbar.com

Ring dings, once merely a mass-marketed grocery snack, have been revolutionized in this establishment. The brainchild of Madeline Lanciani, who is one of TV's *Chopped* champions, has taken the formula of cake the size of a hockey puck, and filled it with fancy creams (Nutella, strawberry cheesecake), and covered it in glazes galore (chocolate, matcha, pistachio).

94 SPOT DESSERT BAR

**13 St Marks Place
(betw 2nd
and 3rd Ave)
East Village ④
+1 212 677 5670**
spotdessertbar.com

Iron Chef Ian Kittichai, has a knack for creating unique, whimsical desserts. Take the Matcha Lava cake, which is served warm, with an oozing green tea ganache inside. Or the Harvest, which is delivered to your table disguised as a potted plant, whose 'dirt' is oreo crumbs topping a raspberry sorbet.

95 POPBAR

**15 West 38th St
(betw 5th and 6th Ave)
Midtown West ⑥
+1 212 444 8141**
pop-bar.com

When you're on the go, it's nice to have something you can eat and walk with. Enter Popbar, with gourmet gelato – made more fun on a stick. Choose your flavor and then decide if you want to dip it in chocolate, caramel corn, crushed waffle cone, or pistachios. Sorbet and yogurt pops too.

The 5 best

CONTINENTAL BRASSERIES

---

96 **THE DUTCH**
131 Sullivan St
(at Prince St)
Soho ②
+1 212 677 6200
thedutchnyc.com

On a cozy Soho corner, the Dutch is a lively spot where folks gather early and late. Oysters, and other raw bar selections, are a big part of the success. They have a nice roster of meat entrees, and a spectacular, albeit pricey, wine list. End your meal with one of the homebaked pies.

97 **MINETTA TAVERN**
113 MacDougal St
(betw Bleecker
and W 3rd St)
Greenwich Village ④
+1 212 475 3850
minettatavernny.com

A restaurant with a long history re-imagined by restaurateur Keith McNally. Almost impossible to get a reservation, it's best to plan a late night supper at the bar. Their burger wins best in New York again and again, falling into the decadent category. Celebs may be spotted here.

98 **THE ODEON**
145 West Broadway
(at Thomas St)
Tribeca ③
+1 212 233 0507
theodeonrestaurant.com

Once the hub of 1980s nightlife and the famous hangout of TV's Saturday Night Live cast, this place continues to attract a fun crowd for brunch, lunch, and dinner. The gorgeous space is donned in a typical bistro-style with paneled walls, high ceilings held up by columns where you can hang your coat on a hook. Try the popular Tuna Burger and some fries.

99 LE CHARLOT

19 East 69th St
(betw Madison
and Park Ave)
Upper East Side ⑦
+1 212 794 6419
lecharlot.us

A taste of Paris in New York. Be ready to rub elbows with the upper east sider at the next table. It's crammed tight with old-school decor, and a classic menu: steak *au poivre*, *patés*, *tartares*, *moules* three ways. If you're looking for something fresh, get the crab salad with avocado and papaya for your appetizer.

100 LE PARISIEN BISTROT

163 East 33rd St
(betw 3rd and
Lexington Ave)
Murray Hill ⑥
+1 212 889 5489
leparisiennyc.com

Small, quaint and *très romantic*: Le Parisien is the perfect intimate neighborhood bistro for a date night. The menu features French comfort food like escargot, mussels, trout, onion soup and crème brûlée, and of course some great wines. A nice place to linger. It's especially popular for brunch.

96 THE DUTCH

5 places to stop at while
GALLERY HOPPING

---

101 FONDA

189 9th Avenue
(at 21st St)
Chelsea ⑤
+1 917 525 5252
fondarestaurant.com

This is the place to go when craving contemporary Mexican comfort food. Chef Roberto Santibañez, from Mexico City, is also traditionally trained at Le Cordon Bleu. His sauces are dense, rich, and plentiful on classics like enchiladas, *flautas de pollo*, and *chile relleno*. Guacamole is made to order. Salads and seafood dishes work for those looking for something lighter.

102 COOKSHOP

156 10th Avenue
(at 20th St)
Chelsea ⑤
+1 212 924 4440
cookshopny.com

This energetic, greenmarket-driven hot spot near the High Line is a perfect place to gird yourself up for gallery hopping in the Chelsea neighborhood. It can get pretty crowded here: everyone loves the uncomplicated American food (breakfast, brunch, lunch and dinner) and the great seating outside along 10th Ave. Book ahead.

103 SHUKETTE

230 9th Avenue
(betw 24th and
25th St)
Chelsea ⑤
+1 212 242 1803
shukettenyc.com

A modern, Middle Eastern hot spot, this is the place for sharing a variety of dips, some of which arrive in technicolor. Locally sourced fresh veggies are the focus, as well as five different breads designed to 'rip'. Finish the meal with an in-house soft serve tahini-flavored ice cream topped with halva floss, hazelnuts, and in-season sour cherries.

104 BOTTINO

246 10th Avenue
(at 24th St)
Chelsea ⑤
+1 212 206 6766
bottinonyc.com

Near the High Line you'll find this art world staple: a very elegant place offering Tuscan dishes and boutique wines. Try to get seated at the comfy banquette with your back against the wall of wines, or choose a table outside in the beautiful garden out back. We like the *tagliata* (seared sliced steak).

105 TÍA POL

205 10th Ave
(at 22nd St)
Chelsea ⑤
+1 212 675 8805
tiapol.com

Rustic and absolutely tiny, this tapas bar takes it up a few notches with traditional Basque dishes. Perfect for a pitstop and light bite at the bar. They are known for their crispy croquettes, which vary daily, and the Spanish-only wine list. Try the lamb skewers and the *patatas bravas*.

5 VEGETARIAN & VEGAN *hotspots*

106 **ABCV**

38 East 19th St
(betw Park Ave S
and Broadway)
Gramercy ⑤
+1 212 475 5829
jean-georges.com

Chef Jean-Georges Vongerichten is expanding his abc empire to include one focused exclusively on vegetables. The decor is funky and fresh, in their inimitable style, with pops of chartreuse. Open for breakfast, lunch and dinner, feast on hearty soups, kabocha squash dip, ancient grain pilaf, and noodle dishes.

107 **CADENCE**

111 East 7th St
(betw 1st Ave and
Ave A)
East Village ④
+1 833 328 4588
*overthrowhospitality.com/
venues/cadence*

Chef Shenarri Freeman interprets southern food classics into new vegan creative soul food masterpieces. A tiny spot with mostly bar seating will have you rubbing elbows with fellow plant lovers to enjoy her smoked grits, maple buttermilk cornbread, collard wraps, and popular Southern Fried Lasagna with red wine *bolognese*, pine nut ricotta, and spinach.

108 DIRT CANDY

**86 Allen St
(betw Grand
and Broome St)
Lower East Side ③
+1 212 228 7732**
dirtcandynyc.com

Chef Amanda Cohen became famous for creating artistic vegetable dishes with the first, tiny outlet of Dirt Candy. Now in a larger airy space downtown, she is able to accommodate her fans. Fun dishes like the super-crunchy, battered Korean fried broccoli can make anyone become a vegetable lover.

109 BLOSSOM

**72 University Place
(betw 10th and 11th St)
Greenwich Village ④
+1 212 627 1144**
*blossomnyc.com/
university*

Totally vegan, but Blossom's menu also appeals to those not following an all-plant diet. The chopped Caesar Salad's crispy shiitake mushrooms taste just like bacon, adding a bit of crunch and lots of wow. The menu includes an unusual mix of veggie-focused dishes with seitan, the beyond burger, and a dynamite pesto pizza. Another location on the Upper West Side.

110 DIVYA'S KITCHEN

**25 1st Avenue
(betw 1st and 2nd St)
Greenwich Village ④
+1 212 477 4834**
divyaskitchen.com

This is where you will get personal interaction from the owner and chef. The almost spiritual atmosphere of this cozy spot is all due to its founder Divya Alter. She is a delightful host and possesses a wealth of knowledge on all things vegan and Ayurvedic. Feel free to order small and large dishes to share and savor.

5 faves from a
NEW YORK FOODIE

---

111 ABC KITCHEN

35 East 18th St
(betw Broadway
and Park Ave)
Gramercy ⑤
+1 212 475 5829
abchome.com

The original ABC that started it all: fresh, lip-smacking dishes with that certain something. Though this place has been open for years, it's still tough to score a reservation, but off-hours are your best shot. As a matter of fact, a brunch here can supply you with tasty fare, plus elixirs that can correct a night of staying out too late.

112 OPHELIA LOUNGE

3 Mitchell Place,
26th Fl.
(corner 1st Ave and
49th St)
Midtown East ⑥
+1 212 980 4796
opheliany.com

We love this place for its gorgeous views and its history. Created as a hotel and club for single women in the 1920s, its penthouse has transformed into the most lovely lounge with wrap-around terrace. A fun spot for cocktails and small plates enjoyed in a stunning art deco-setting with velvet banquettes. Thursday through Saturday nights feature DJs.

113 PORTALE

126 West 18th St
(betw 6th and 7th Ave)
Chelsea ⑤
+1 917 781 0255
portalerestaurant.com

Chef Alfred Portale revolutionized upscale eating in Manhattan in the 80s at Gotham. Here he brings a wonderful seasonality to Italian dishes, with unexpected twists and extraordinary ingredients. Situated in a fresh, minimalist mid-century style environment, you will feel pampered. The shaved cauliflower salad is a great way to start your meal. Order the duck if it's something you enjoy, it is sensational.

114 THE CAMPBELL

AT: GRAND CENTRAL
STATION
15 Vanderbilt Avenue
(betw 42nd and
43rd St)
Midtown East ⑥
+1 917 209 3440
thecampbellnyc.com

Here's another NYC landmark with stunning design and a cool history. It's an upscale spot where those commuting from Grand Central will stop in for a cocktail before getting on the train. A wonderful spot to consider for a late lunch (or early drinks) or dinner. Bar bites only. Stand at the bar to mingle. There is a dress code.

115 WICKED JANE

15 West 8th St
(betw 5th and 6th Ave)
Greenwich Village ④
+1 646 329 5767
wickedjane.com

Their artistically prepared small plates appeal to all the senses with sauces you will want to lap up. Try the refreshing Raw Live Scallops and the perfectly pastel Lightly Cooked Salmon. Wicked Jane's sparsely designed space gives you room to breathe, with a fun soundtrack. Solo diners can eat at the bar.

5 restaurants for
SEAFOOD

---

116 **THE FULTON**
AT: SOUTH STREET
SEAPORT
89 South St
Financial District ①
+1 212 838 1200
thefulton.nyc

You can't beat The Fulton's expansive views of the East River and Lower Manhattan bridges. The food happens to match the superb views with dishes that are inventive and extraordinarily fresh with sensational sauces. The dining room has a nautical vibe with roomy seating inside and out.

117 **TACOMBI**
AT: FONDA NOLITA
267 Elizabeth St
(betw Prince
and Houston St)
Nolita ③
+1 917 727 0179
tacombi.com

Set up in a raw garage with skylight and its kitchen inside a VW bus, Tacombi is a spot serving home-style Mexican food with sustainable ingredients. Park yourself at one of their card tables on a metal folding chair to enjoy crispy fish tacos supreme and lip-smacking ceviches in a most festive environment.

118 **LURE FISHBAR**
142 Mercer St
(at Prince St)
Soho ②
+1 212 431 7676
lurefishbar.com

Housed in a space resembling a fine yacht, thereby accentuating their focus on the sea world. Though this spot has been there a while, it still attracts a cool crowd looking to sample raw bar goodies, sushi rolls, clam chowders, and perfectly executed fish entrees.

119 FLEX MUSSELS

154 West 13th St
(betw 6th and 7th Ave)
Greenwich Village ④
+1 212 229 0222
flexmussels.com

Slurp some mussels here, offered in four flavor profiles: white wine, creamy, tomato, and their exotic signature sauce. Start out with cornmeal-crusted clam strips, or fried oysters with spicy aioli for dipping. The space has a simple feel of a whited-out barn with pitched roof and farm landscape. Second location on the Upper East Side.

120 KYMA

15 West 18th St
(betw 5th and 6th Ave)
Flatiron ⑤
+1 212 268 5555
kymarestaurants.com

A boisterous spot with extremely fresh seafood shipped from the Mediterranean daily and prepared simply to let the ingredients shine. This Greek restaurant features memorable dishes like tuna tartare with crispy potatoes, dollops of yogurt and avocado mousse; tender octopus; and baked sesame-crusted feta in a cherry sauce. Lunch, brunch, dinner.

120 KYMA

5 top
TASTING MENUS

---

121 NICHE NICHE

43 MacDougal St
(betw King and
W Houston St)
Soho ②
nichenichenyc.com

From the founder of Air's Champagne Parlor comes this dinner party concept with a focus on wine. Four courses, four wines, for 88 dollars. The menu changes nightly, Monday through Friday, based on the wines that have been hand-picked by the guest sommelier. A max of 25 guests makes it intimate. After 10 pm a live music lounge below opens with sounds of blues, soul and jazz.

122 63 CLINTON

63 Clinton St
(betw Stanton and
Rivington St)
Lower East Side ③
+1 917 663 6223
63clinton.com

A pair of chefs formerly at Chef's Table at Brooklyn Fare opened this intimate space highlighting a seven-course tasting menu. Each meal starts with their breakfast taco which sets the tone with its arty presentation and elevated techniques. The room is rustic and inviting, in a minimalist sort of way. A nice upscale find in this neighborhood.

123 THE MUSKET ROOM

265 Elizabeth St
(betw Prince and
Houston St)
Nolita ③
+1 212 219 0764
musketroom.com

A handsomely rustic dining experience complemented by a lovely, backyard garden with seating. The space looks comfortably informal, but the dishes that arrive are meticulously styled – and the flavors are wonderfully unexpected and globally inspired. A vegan tasting is also an option.

124 GABRIEL KREUTHER

41 West 42nd St
(betw 5th and 6th Ave)
Midtown ⑥
+1 212 257 5826
gknyc.com

The Alsatian chef, formerly of The Modern, is running the show here in the most sophisticated way. The space is divided into two sections, with a more casual menu at the bar. For a special night, opt for the 4-course *prix fixe* in the main dining room, and be lovingly treated to beautifully styled dishes with his signature touch.

125 THE MODERN

AT: MOMA
9 West 53rd St
(betw 5th and 6th Ave)
Midtown ⑥
+1 212 333 1220
themodernnyc.com

We love dining in The Bar Room, but if you are looking for a meal to remember, book a dinner in the dining room that overlooks MoMA's sculpture garden. Service is impeccable, along with the artsy plates and silverware customized to each course. Dress up. For true foodies, book The Kitchen Table, where the chef prepares a bespoke menu.

CAFFE REGGIO

70 PLACES
FOR A DRINK

---

5 places to fuel up with **COFFEE** —————— 84

5 places to sip cocktails in **LUX** setting —————— 86

5 opulent spots for experiencing **HIGH TEA** —————— 88

5 thought-provoking bars for **INTELLECTUALS** —— 90

5 places to get **COFFEE** and **LINGER** —————— 92

The 5 best places to enjoy a **BEER** —————— 94

5 great old-school **BARS** —————— 96

The 5 best **HOTEL** and **ROOFTOP BARS** —————— 98

5 places for **OENOPHILES** —————— 100

5 funky bars on the **LOWER EAST SIDE** —————— 102

5 great places for **ARTISANAL COCKTAILS** —— 104

5 places to watch **F O O T B A L L** *(the Euro kind)* —— 106

5 places with a **P E R S O N A L I T Y** *all their own* —— 108

5 places to get drinks
P R E *or* **A P R E S   T H E A T E R** ———————— 110

5 places to fuel up with
COFFEE

126 **TARALLUCCI E VINO**

15 East 18th St
(betw 5th Ave
and Broadway)
Union Square ⑤
+1 212 228 5400
tarallucievino.net

This is a true-Italian, upscale spot, where you can drink your shot their way, standing at the counter. Iced espresso, made the proper way – by shaking, can be had, along with a full breakfast menu and pastries. It's open all day, so you can switch to wine later, or stop for a sandwich, or dinner. 3 other locations.

127 **JOE COFFEE**

141 Waverly Place
(at Gay St)
West Village ④
+1 212 924 6750
joenewyork.com

On one of the quaintest corners in the village are two benches where you can take in the NYC *Zeitgeist* as you relax and sip your morning Joe. The art of coffee is taken seriously here, with staff trained to be proper baristas, and where they roast their proprietary blend. 9 other locations.

128 **BLUESTONE LANE**

1114 6th Avenue
(at W 43rd St)
Midtown ⑥
+1 212 764 0044
bluestonelaneny.com

A nice pitstop on your midtown touring schedule. Located across from Bryant Park and in the courtyard of the Grace building lies this rustic departure. This Australian coffee chain offers Melbourne fare for snacking: like avocado with a tahini twist, or their P.L.A.T. (prosciutto, lettuce, avocado, and tomato).

129 **CULTURE ESPRESSO**
72 West 38th St
(betw 5th and 6th Ave)
Times Square ⑥
+1 212 302 0200
cultureespresso.com

In a charming, high-ceiling space, this independently owned coffee shop is a great find in a section of town not known for amenities. Their coffee of choice come from Heart Coffee Roasters of Portland, who process their beans preserving all the tasty nuances. Pair your brew with their famous chocolate chip cookies to fuel your city wanderings. Wi-Fi available.

130 **LA COLOMBE COFFEE ROASTERS**
400 Lafayette St
(at 4th St)
Noho ④
+1 212 677 5834
lacolombe.com

In a majestic sun-filled space, sip extra-ordinary coffee sourced around the globe. They're known for their roasting and blends, and for being the inventors of latte on draft: a cold-pressed espresso with frothed milk served cold (also available in cans for toting). You will encounter a line, but it moves quickly. Five other locations.

127 **JOE COFFEE**

5 places to sip cocktails in
L U X *setting*

---

131 DEAR IRVING ON HUDSON
AT: ALIZ HOTEL TIMES SQ,
40TH AND 41ST FL.
**310 West 40th St
Times Square ⑥**
dearirving.com

This brand has expanded to Midtown, with glamorous digs and expansive views. Enjoy their assortment of top-notch cocktails in a sleek, plush setting with paneled lacquered walls and velvety sofas. They even offer cocktail classes, so you can learn the secrets behind their well-balanced cocktails. Tempting bar snacks are also available.

132 SWEET POLLY
**71 6th Avenue
(betw Flatbush Ave
and Bergen St)
Prospect Heights,
Brooklyn ⑪
+1 718 484 9600**
sweetpollynyc.com

High, embossed gold ceilings, a gorgeous living plant wall, and sleek mirrors set the mood for its upscale clientele. Sit at the elegant white marble bar with old fashioned lamps that subtlely illuminate your cocktails. Order a Dirty Martini on tap, or get the night going with a kick of caffeine in The Golden Eye.

133 CLOVER CLUB

**210 Smith St
(betw Baltic
and Butler St)
Cobble Hill,
Brooklyn** ⑪
+1 718 855 7939
cloverclubny.com

Two vibes: In the back, an elegant wood-paneled lounge with beamed mirrored ceilings mixed with Louis XIV chairs, 70s chandeliers, and a cozy fireplace. Up front, the vintage mahogany bar is where carefully prepared pre-Prohibition drinks are created: a variety of fizzes, smashes, swizzles and sours. Live jazz, and a neighborhood feeling waft through.

134 LE BOUDOIR

**135 Atlantic Avenue
(betw Henry
and Clinton St)
Brooklyn Heights,
Brooklyn** ⑩
+1 347 227 8337
boudoirbk.com

In a space that was once part of the Atlantic Avenue tunnel lies an opulent fantasy, styled after Marie Antionette's private rooms. Think plush red velvet booths and ornate mirrors. Enter through the bookcase door of their upstairs spot Chez Moi, for decadent cocktails like the Dauphin: absinthe, chile liqueur, almond milk, coconut, cacao nibs.

135 ELSIE ROOFTOP

**1412 Broadway
(betw 39th and
40th St)
Midtown West** ⑥
+1 646 834 2291
elsierooftop.com

In 1920s flair, a bar inspired by interior designer and socialite Elsie de Wolfe sits atop 25 stories close to Bryant Park. Outdoor space surrounds the penthouse, nestled in by Midtown towers, which gets glassed in during colder months. Fun and raucous. Saturday High Tea with burlesque. Only open Wednesday to Sunday.

5 opulent spots for experiencing
H I G H   T E A

---

136 LADY MENDL'S
56 Irving Place
(betw 17th and 18th St)
Gramercy ⑤
+1 212 533 4600
ladymendlsteasalon.com

Look for the small teacup on the brass plaque near the front door to uncover this modern take on traditional afternoon tea. Lady Mendl's presents an opulent five courses – soup/salad, finger sandwiches, scones, and lots of sweets – served on mismatched china in the most striking and authentic Georgian brownstone. Reservations required: from Thursday to Friday, 1 to 4 pm and Saturday to Sunday, 12 to 5 pm.

137 PRINCE TEA HOUSE
204 East 10th St
(betw 1st and 2nd Ave)
East Village ④
+1 917 388 2778
princeteahouse.com

Slow down and experience opulent French style with Asian sensibility. This afternoon tea comes with your choice of tea from their extensive selections, with unlimited refill for two hours, accompanied by assorted mini pastries, scones, and five different finger sandwiches. Tea is kept lovingly warm with accompanying tea light. Six more locations in NYC.

138 PEMBROKE ROOM

AT: THE LOWELL HOTEL
**28 East 63rd St
(betw Madison and
Park Ave)
Upper East Side ⑦
+1 212 605 6825**
*lowellhotel.com/
restaurants-and-bar/
pembroke-room*

Head up the marble staircase to arrive at a British-inspired salon with glittering crystal, polished silver and lace curtains. Expect the highest standards while enjoying warm scones with Devonshire cream and lemon curd, five tea sandwiches, and sweets. Add a glass of sherry, wine or champagne and caviar to make it that much more special. Make sure to reserve, Wednesday to Sunday from 2 to 6 pm.

139 THE WHITBY BAR

AT: THE WHITBY HOTEL
**18 West 56th St
(betw 5th and 6th Ave)
Midtown West ⑥
+1 212 586 5656**
*firmdalehotels.com/
hotels/new-york/
the-whitby-hotel*

You would expect a British brand of hotels to get afternoon tea right – and they do: a selection of ten teas served on whimsical Wedgwood china with creative finger sandwiches, house-made scones with clotted cream and a myriad of desserts will thrill traditionalists. The light-filled Orangery Room is as charming as it gets. Add a glass of bubbly for extra sparkle.

140 MAD HATTERS (GIN &) TEA PARTY

**330 Madison Avenue
(betw 42nd and
43rd St)
Midtown East ⑥**
*madhatter
ginteaparty.com*

For those into dress-up and immersive events comes a tea party à la Alice in Wonderland. You won't be getting tea in your tea cups here, but a mix of gin cocktails and lots of weird and wonderful entertainment. This trip down the rabbit hole lasts one and a half hours hosted by a team of actors devoted to making your evening fun. No food, 21 and over to attend.

5 thought-provoking bars for
INTELLECTUALS

---

141 NYC TRIVIA LEAGUE
nyctrivialeague.com

This league hosts Trivia Nights in venues all over the city. Check out their website to see which bars are hosting every night of the week. Register your team of six for free, and plan to play every week. For the truly competitive, the season lasts 10 to 12 weeks, with major prizes offered for the team with the highest score. Play is also virtual.

142 CAVEAT
21-A Clinton St
(betw Stanton
and Houston St)
Lower East Side ③
+1 212 228 2100
caveat.nyc

Caveat is the place where intellectual talks and performances are held, while you sit at long tables with a craft beer or cocktail. There are storytellers, science fairs for adults, team trivia contests, fun SAT tests with bar room knowledge, food factoids, and philosophy – a real mixed bag of eclectic acts to choose from.

143 KGB BAR

85 East 4th St
(betw 2nd Ave
and Bowery)
East Village ④
+1 212 505 3360
kgbbar.com

KGB Bar has long serviced literary types in its red walled divey space. Regular readings have taken place here since the early 1990s. In the Red Room upstairs you can see performances, storytelling, poetry readings, with Sundays set aside for fiction read by emerging writers. Check the calendar for almost daily events.

144 THE EAR INN

326 Spring St
(betw Greenwich
and Washington St)
Tribeca ③
+1 212 226 9060
theearinn.com

One of the oldest bars in New York. The name comes from its famous neon sign, where part of the letter B in BAR is missing. Creative types mingle with regulars and listen to live music, which happens three nights a week, along with poetry readings and film screenings, fed by an elevated farm-to-table bar menu.

145 THE DEAD POET

450 Amsterdam Ave
(betw 81st and
82nd St)
Upper West Side ⑦
+1 212 595 5670
thedeadpoet.com

Experience a bevy of cocktails inspired by famous poets and authors, including a seasonal reading list – while getting inspiration for your next read. Their most popular cocktail, the Dead Poet, incorporates seven liquors with a splash of sour mix that ends up tasting like grape soda – you get to keep the glass as a souvenir. Best spot for a perfect pour of Guinness.

5 places to get
COFFEE and LINGER

---

146 MAMAN
239 Centre St
(betw Grand
and Broome St)
Soho ②
+1 212 226 0700
mamannyc.com

The brainchild of a Michelin chef, a mixologist, and a baker, this charming spot is absolutely picture-perfect, as witnessed on their Instagram page. Sit near the open kitchen or spread out in the pleasant back room. Known for their tartinettes and crispy-on-the-outside-soft-on-the-inside-cookies. 11 other locations.

147 STUMPTOWN

147 STUMPTOWN

30 West 8th St
(at MacDougal St)
Greenwich Village ④
+1 855 711 3385
stumptowncoffee.com

This location epitomizes the clean and modern Stumptown aesthetic, with exposed brick walls, long benches, and an attractive parquet floor. Located on the stretch of 8th Street that is coming back to life with new and exciting venues, it's a quiet space you can linger in.

148 HI-COLLAR

231 East 9th St
(betw 1st and 2nd Ave)
East Village ④
+1 212 777 7018
hi-collar.com

A sweet, zen Japanese place inspired by kissaten (old-school Japanese coffee shops). Grab a stool and try their famous extra fluffy pancakes along with a coffee, which is brewed precisely in a siphon and served in pretty ceramic tea cups. At night they switch their focus to sake.

149 CAFFE REGGIO

119 MacDougal St
(betw W 3rd
and Bleecker St)
Greenwich Village ④
+1 212 475 9557
caffereggio.com

Where cappuccino was introduced to America in 1927, this spot is a true Village piece of history with its original ornamental espresso machine preserved on display. Its old-world atmosphere still attracts the latest generation of creative thinkers. Sit outside at one of the small round tables and watch the world go by.

150 THE WELL

52 East 15th St
(betw Union Square
West and 5th Ave)
Union Square ⑤
+1 646 560 8080
the-well.com

A hop, skip and a jump from Union Square houses a wellness retreat that features a spa, yoga studio, pilates, meditation classes, and their cafe, Kitchen & Table. Head here before or after treatments, or just enjoy the all-day menu of healthy goodies and the best coffees, teas, and cleansing juices.

The 5 best places to enjoy a
B E E R

---

151 **COVENHOVEN**
730 Classon Avenue
(betw Park and
Prospect Pl)
Prospect Heights,
Brooklyn ⑪
+1 718 483 9950
covenhovennyc.com

A few blocks from the Brooklyn Museum is a beer mecca featuring 16 frequently changing taps in addition to their collection of 250+ bottles and cans. If that weren't enough, they have a lovely plant-filled garden – with grass – and monthly events showcasing a brewer or unusual brand. Gourmet selection of grilled cheese, plus sausages and pretzels. They also offer wine.

152 **TORCH & CROWN**
12 Vandam St
(betw 6th Ave and
Varick St)
Soho ②
+1 212 228 7005
torchandcrown.com

A 9000-square-foot industrial brewing company right in Manhattan that mixes long bar-top tables and places to mingle indoors and out. The menu currently offers 18 varieties accredited to Torch & Crown. Investigate their special events like the oyster/dark beer happy hour or two-hour beer tours of the city. Small plates, salads and sandwiches and a steak accompany the brews.

153 TØRST

**615 Manhattan Ave
(betw Nassau and
Driggs Ave)
Greenpoint,
Brooklyn** ⑨
+1 718 389 6034
torstnyc.com

Opened by Jeppe Jarnit-Bjergso, a Danish brewer, and Daniel Burns, once head of Momofuku's test kitchen. The space resembles a minimalist beer lab, a mix of cool white marble and reclaimed wood panels. Beer pours from 21 taps using a specialized system ensuring your brew comes out at the correct temperature.

154 BLIND TIGER

**281 Bleecker St
(at Jones St)
Greenwich Village** ④
+1 212 462 4682
blindtigeralehouse.com

A microbrewery stationed on the part of Bleecker street away from the upscale boutiques. Twenty-eight beers on tap compete with their bottled beer selections, which are divided into categories like Sours & Funk, and Barrel-aged, plus some really special picks. Accompany your chugging with their Grilled 5 Cheese sandwich.

155 TOP HOPS BEER SHOP

AT: ESSEX MARKET
**88 Essex St
(betw Delancey and
Broome St)
Lower East Side** ③
+1 917 261 2561
tophops.com/top-hops-at-essex-market

Inside this fabulous food mart is a specialty beer mecca with a selection of 70 bottles and cans plus 6 lines on tap, and also wine and small bites. Their daily featured guest beers highlight seasonal offerings from local breweries including Industrial Arts, Lawson's and Other Half. Great place to support small local NYC enterprises.

5 great
OLD-SCHOOL BARS

---

156 OLD TOWN BAR

**45 East 18th St
(betw Broadway
and Park Ave)
Union Square** ⑤
+1 212 529 6732
oldtownbar.com

Old Town is a bar set up as real bars are meant to be: a no-nonsense, no music, beer-swilling brouhaha. High ceilings create a feeling of space, mosaic tile floors are classic (as are the marble pissoirs in the men's room). Go one flight up to order one of the best burgers in town.

157 WALKER'S

**16 North Moore St
(at Varick St)
Tribeca** ③
+1 212 941 0142
walkerstribeca.com

A neighborhood bar with locals and guys-in-suits-come-to-loosen-their-ties, remains a slice of this neighborhood's working-class past. Housing a well-worn bar and cool photos of Tribeca's past, this is the spot for a draft beer or whiskey and good (stiff) regular cocktails.

158 FANELLI CAFE

**94 Prince St
(at Mercer St)
Soho** ②
+1 212 226 9412
fanellicafe.nyc

Soho, in all its fashionableness, still embraces this character-filled hold out (since 1847). Squeeze in at the bar, where you might end up talking to a leftover resident artist from the 80s, or at one of the red-and-white checkered tablecloth tables. Staff comes with NY attitude to complete the picture.

159 PETE'S TAVERN

**129 East 18th St
(at Irving Pl)
Gramercy ⑤
+1 212 473 7676**
petestavern.com

The site of NYC's oldest bar and restaurant, this spot still houses the 40-foot rosewood bar, tin ceiling and tile floors from 1864. Hang out at the very popular bar or enjoy American and Italian specialties in the 'locked-in-time' dining room, in which O. Henry penned *Gift of the Magi* in one of the booths. Monday to Friday happy hour from 4 to 6 pm.

160 P.J. CLARKE'S

**915 3rd Avenue
(at 55th St)
Midtown East ⑥
+1 212 317 1616**
pjclarkes.com

This place still has the cachet of the original bar which became a star-studded establishment. It's a spot that is always buzzing and fun, so if you want to get into a New York groove, this is the place. Accompany your classic or creative cocktail with some oysters, fish & chips, lobster roll, chicken pot pie or a short rib stew.

156 OLD TOWN BAR

The 5 best
HOTEL and ROOFTOP
BARS

---

161 BAR HUGO
525 Greenwich St
(betw Spring and
Vandam St)
Soho ③
+1 917 409 2581
barhugorooftop.com

This rooftop bar has views of a different sort. Focused on the Hudson River and Downtown, you can enjoy a magical sunset, which gives the space a beautiful glow before all the city lights come on. Here you can sip on very creative cocktails, while listening to a great music mix. Come early to get a spot.

162 BEMELMANS BAR
AT: THE CARLYLE HOTEL
35 East 76th St
(at Madison Ave)
Upper East Side ⑦
+1 212 744 1600
rosewoodhotels.com

Red jacketed waiters remind us of the long lost New York iconized by Frank Sinatra. Settle in at the bar for a night to remember, and chat up the Upper East Side clientele. Woody Allen plays on Tuesdays at this spot where live jazz dominates. Pricey cover charge after 9 pm.

163 TEMPLE COURT
AT: THE BEEKMAN HOTEL
5 Beekman St
(betw Park Row
and Nassau St)
Financial District ①
+1 212 658 1848
templecourtnyc.com

One of the most astounding spaces to sip a cocktail in NYC, inside a breathtaking nine-story Victorian atrium. In this landmarked 1883 Gothic Revival building, the bar is a study in gold and green, with old-fashioned iron stools, and lighting via small lamps. Get a table and luxuriate in the comfortable opulence.

164 GALLOW GREEN

AT: THE MCKITTRICK HOTEL
**530 West 27th St
(betw 10th and
11th Ave)
Chelsea** ⑤
+1 212 564 1662
*mckittrickhotel.com/
gallow-green*

Total scene above the place famous for the immersive theater experience *Sleep No More*. Less about views and more about a lush escape from the city. Decked out in greenery and backyard patio lights in summer, dolled up like a log cabin in winter – with amazing attention to detail. Earlier is better, if you want to gain access.

165 THE BAR

AT: THE BACCARAT HOTEL
**28 West 53rd St
(at 5th Ave)
Midtown East** ⑥
+1 866 957 5139
baccarathotels.com

Down the block from MoMA, B Bar is as stunningly beautiful as a palace, with elaborate namesake crystal chandeliers everywhere you look. At the bar, you may snag one of the bar stools for two (which seem to be popping up more and more). Cocktails will be elegantly presented in iconic Baccarat cut crystal glassware.

162 **BEMELMANS BAR**

5 places for

OENOPHILES

---

166 **LA COMPAGNIE DES VINS SURNATURELS**

249 Centre St (betw Broome and Grand St)
Soho ②
+1 212 343 3660
compagnienyc.com

This is a serious wine bar which loves to educate and delight wine lovers in a rustic, low-lit setting. They feature an unusual mix of 750+ wines from around the world. French small bites, charcuterie and cheese are on the menu. Sign up for the themed Wine Boot Camp classes for four tastes with food pairing.

166 LA COMPAGNIE DES VINS SURNATURELS

167 AIR'S CHAMPAGNE PARLOR

**127 MacDougal St
(betw 4th and 3rd St)
Greenwich Village** ④
+1 212 420 4777
*airschampagne
parlor.com*

Let the sommelier guide you through the sparkling world of flavors at this champagne-only bar. It's an adorable art deco parlor with a world assortment of affordable to splurgy bottles. Accompany sips with creamy oysters, a luscious *crudo* (like the salmon in pesto), or some crispy truffle frites.

168 FIG.19

**131 Chrystie St
(betw Broome
and Kenmare St)
Lower East Side** ③
figurenineteen.com

Hidden behind a door at the end of an art gallery lies a cool, raw space with chandeliers and fireplace. Noteworthy: Fig.19 has prosecco on tap, and it's a place that always attracts a lively, indie, artsy crowd at all hours.

169 BROOKLYN WINERY WINE BAR

**213 North 8th St
(betw Driggs
and Roebling St)
Williamsburg,
Brooklyn** ⑨
+1 347 763 1506
bkwinery.com

One of two full-fledged winemaking facilities in NYC, Brooklyn Winery produces about 16 varieties in their picturesque space (which hosts many a wedding). Get a taste of the signature wines at the wine bar, by the glass or bottle. Flights allow you to sample 3 different varietals, like the NY State Trio, or Chardonnay 3 Ways.

170 ALDO SOHM WINE BAR

**151 West 51st St
(betw 6th and 7th Ave)
Midtown West** ⑥
+1 212 554 1143
aldosohmwinebar.com

This is like being in Aldo's comfortable living room. The longtime sommelier of Le Bernardin has set up shop next door, off a mall in the middle of 51st Street, offering (more) affordable wines and small plates. For something really special, be there for Aldo After Dark, when he opens his daily magnums at 4 pm.

5 funky bars on the
LOWER EAST SIDE

---

171 SUBJECT
**188 Suffolk St
(betw E Houston and
Stanton St)
Lower East Side ③
+1 646 422 7898**
subject-les.com

Here's a relaxed, welcoming place that produces totally creative cocktails. They are passionate about making their own sodas, bitters, and syrups, so you know you'll be getting quality libations. When hunger hits, they offer a couple sandwiches (one vegan), snacks, and boozy cupcakes to complete the picture. Colorful outdoor seating. Reservations are encouraged.

172 THE BACK ROOM
**102 Norfolk St
(betw Delancey and
Rivington St)
Lower East Side ③
+1 212 228 5098**
backroomnyc.com

One of only two remaining operating speakeasies in Manhattan, whose clientele included mobsters from the 1920s, retains its original vintage vibe. Walk through the gate, down the stairs and through a long covered walkway to reach the entrance. Their artisanal cocktails are served in teacups, as was done in the past. Bottle service available.

173 HOME SWEET HOME

**131 Chrystie St
(betw Broome
and Delancey St)
Lower East Side ③
+1 212 226 5709
*www.homesweet
homebar.com***

Taxidermy enthusiasts will get their fill here in this space outfitted almost like a curiosity shop. If you like to dance, you've come to the right dive bar. They've got a lounge with a dance floor and the DJs play a quirky mix of 50s-90s-swing. Dancing usually starts after 10 pm.

174 MARSHALL STACK

**66 Rivington St
(at Allen St)
Lower East Side ③
+1 212 228 4667
*@marshallstacknyc***

A true LES gem that has an extra long bar with a great selection of decently priced bottled beers. A mishmash interior of painted white brick mixes with exposed plaster and painted tin ceilings, with a 1950s-style jukebox (!) full of righteous rock tunes. Bar food, like Sliders and Tilapia Po' Boys can be had too.

175 WELCOME TO THE JOHNSON'S

**123 Rivington St
(betw Norfolk
and Essex St)
Lower East Side ③
+1 212 420 9911
*@jholetv***

A dive in every sense of the word, from its sticker-covered old brown refrigerator holding 2-dollar Pabst Blue Ribbons and plastic-covered sofas. Imagine the 1970s basement of heroin addicts, complete with layers of graffiti covering every inch of the bathroom walls. They boast killer Bloody Marys and a pool table too.

5 great places for
ARTISANAL COCKTAILS

---

176 **HOLIDAY COCKTAIL LOUNGE**
**75 St Marks Place
(betw 2nd
and 3rd Ave)
East Village** ④
+1 212 777 9637
*holidaycocktail
lounge.nyc*

For nearly 100 years, this space attracted notables with personality (Madonna, Sinatra, Keith Richards, Iggy Pop, Allen Ginsburg, Trotsky). The recent modern-with-kitsch makeover retains a vintage feel. Cocktails are cultivated by brothers Michael and Danny Neff, who are committed to honoring its gritty, celebrity-studded past.

177 **MARTINY'S**
**121 East 17th St
(betw Union Square
East and Irving Pl)
Union Square** ⑤

A former bartender from Angel's Share (a beloved Japanese bar in the East Village now closed) has created a cocktail den in a sweet carriage house. This is a truly upscale, intimate experience steeped in the rules of Japanese hospitality. The upstairs focus is on whiskies.

178 ANALOGUE

**19 West 8th St
(betw 5th and 6th Ave)
Greenwich Village** ④
+1 212 432 0200
analoguenyc.com

Enjoy your artisanal cocktail with the sounds of live Brazilian jazz in the background. The space is set up in a modern, clean style, with long leather banquettes lining one side of the room. As with most cocktail driven bars, the menu changes with the seasons, and they'll make a special concoction just for you.

179 KATANA KITTEN

**531 Hudson St
(betw Charles and
W 10th St)
West Village** ④
+1 347 866 7739
katanakitten.com

Innovative, upscale versions of beer-and-a-shot boilermakers by Masahiro Urushido, whose Japanese heritage influences both the cocktails and the food. Cocktails include ingredients like matcha, shiso, hinoki tree essence, and sake. Crinkle cut fries come with nori seaweed sprinkled on top. The music is loud here, adding to the raucous vibe.

180 ATTABOY

**134 Eldridge St
(betw Broome
and Delancey St)
Lower East Side** ③
+1 855 877 9900
attaboys.us

In the former Milk & Honey space, two of its former bartenders have set up a new place to sip cocktails. An expanded bar and narrow booths line the laidback white brick space. No menu: you are invited to describe what you like. No reservations: ring the buzzer next to the steel door with "AB" to get in.

5 places to watch
F O O T B A L L
(the Euro kind)

---

181 **SMITHFIELD HALL NYC**
**138 West 25th St
(betw 6th and 7th Ave)
Chelsea ⑤
+1 212 929 9677**
smithfieldnyc.com

This popular place aims to please, stating if you don't see your soccer game on their schedule, they will try and get it on. In addition to soccer, their TVs feature American football, hockey, basketball, baseball and rugby games, so sports fanatics can find any reason to stop by. They serve both cocktails and beer by the pitcher with 18 beers on tap.

183 **BONSIGNOUR**

182 BXL CAFÉ

**125 West 43rd St
(betw 6th Ave and
Broadway)
Midtown** ⑥
+1 212 768 0200
www.bxlrestaurants.com

Jules is the quintessential restaurant/
bar owner – don't think we've ever seen
him in a bad mood. This is where you
can escape from the craziness of Times
Square, and nurse yourself with football
and food: Belgian beer and all-you-can-eat
moules frites. In Flatiron try his BXL Zoute
on 50 W 22nd Street.

183 BONSIGNOUR

**35 Jane St
(at 8th Ave)
West Village** ④
+1 212 229 9700
@bonsignourcafe

Not a real football place unless you come
during the European or World football
cups when you can watch TV on the street
with fellow fans. Hot & cold sandwiches,
paninis and a stacked fridge. Sit on the
bench in front and you're in Old Europe.

184 LEGENDS

**6 West 33rd St
(betw 5th and 6th Ave)
Midtown West** ⑥
+1 212 967 7792
legends33.com

This place is THE place to go to see any
soccer game. Check the schedule on the
website to see who's playing. Many of the
games are in the morning and afternoon,
due to the time change – so you know
you are watching live. The space has
20 big screen TVs and covers all the major
European and South American leagues.

185 MUSTANG HARRY'S

**352 7th Avenue
(betw 29th and
30th St)
Chelsea** ⑤
+1 212 268 8930
*www.mustang
harrys.com*

This expansive space, steps from Madison
Square Garden, is a mecca for sports
enthusiasts. Their 99-foot bar boasts
16 TVs tuned into the latest popular game.
Fare and service deliver much more that
you would expect. Beer lovers, order
a growler and you can take it to go.

5 places with a
PERSONALITY
all their own

---

186 SID GOLD'S REQUEST ROOM
165 West 26th St
(betw 6th and 7th Ave)
Chelsea ⑤
+1 212 229 1948
sidgolds.com

Glitzy, as in Las Vegas, with kitschy 1950s barware and memorabilia. Karaoke singing goes on in the back around a grand piano. Guest pianists with different leanings will play whatever you request, see song lists online. Reservations encouraged, as space is limited.

187 THE UNCOMMONS
230 Thompson St
(betw Bleecker
and W 3rd St)
Greenwich Village ④
+1 646 543 9215
uncommonsnyc.com

For those who love to play games, literally. Inside is an entire wall stacked with over 1200 board games (Monopoly, Backgammon, Risk, and other obscure titles). For 10 dollars you can go in and play all the games you want. Coffee, tea – plus beer, wine, and cider.

188 BROOKLYN BOWL
61 Wythe Avenue
(betw N 11th
and 12th St)
Williamsburg,
Brooklyn ⑨
+1 718 963 3369
brooklynbowl.com

The triple threat: a music venue, bar, and upscale sixteen lane bowling-alley – which sits right next to where live acts, like Guns N' Roses and Elvis Costello, have played. Acts include the latest indy bands, novelty shows, and a weekly spin by DJ Questlove. Great fried chicken supplied by a NYC favorite, Blue Ribbon.

189 MARIE'S CRISIS CAFÉ

**59 Grove St
(betw 7th Ave S
and Bleecker)
West Village ④
+1 212 243 9323
mariescrisiscafe.com**

A show tune sing-along place filled with enthusiastic, diehard fans. Mostly gay men (though all theater lovers come and are welcome) surround a piano in an underground spot, and beautifully belt out one show tune after the other, while drinking from plastic cups. It's a joyful spot that dates back to the early 1900s.

190 THE STONEWALL INN

**53 Christopher St
(at 7th Ave)
Greenwich Village ④
+1 212 488 2705
thestonewallinnnyc.com**

The site of the riots in 1969, and now a National Landmark. A rite of passage for many gay men, it's a short walk from Washington Square Park – you'll recognize it by its iconic arched red brick facade, neon sign, and rainbow flags waving. Afternoon drinking encouraged with 2-for-1 drinks between 2 and 7.30 pm.

190 THE STONEWALL INN

5 places to get drinks **PRE** or **APRES THEATER**

191 **THE RUM HOUSE**
AT: HOTEL EDISON
**228 West 47th St
(betw 7th and 8th Ave)
Times Square** ⑥
therumhousenyc.com

If you are looking for drama, sophistication, and a damn good rum cocktail look no further. This place would be popular no matter its location, but having this gem in Times Square is a godsend. Nightly live piano and jazz and exemplary cocktails keep people crowding in to enjoy a wonderful vibe and camaraderie. No reservations. Snacks only.

192 **TANNER SMITHS**
**204 West 55th St
(betw 7th and 8th Ave)
Times Square** ⑥
+1 646 590 2034
tannersmiths.com

This place seems almost carved out of the New York underground with its woody, antique vibe and sensible and warm service. Two floors specialize in barrel-aged drinks, smoked numbers, and standard fare. For ambiance, TVs play old black and white movies, not sports. Live music on Saturday brunch, DJs on Friday night.

193 HURLEY'S SALOON
232 West 48th St
(betw 7th and 8th Ave)
Times Square ⑥
+1 212 765 8981
hurleysnyc.com

The best part about this place is that it has three floors and will be steps away from most Broadway shows. It is a down-to-earth spot, bearing an Irish pub dynamic with dark paneling, Victorian wallpaper, and red leather. Seasonal outdoor tables available on the heated rooftop. Pints and Guinness and great martinis.

194 ARDESIA WINE BAR
510 West 52nd St
(betw 10th and
11th Ave)
Hell's Kitchen ⑥
+1 212 247 9191
ardesia-ny.com

A cool, high-ceiling room with super tall blackboard toting the over 25 wines by the glass and a menu of 60+ affordable bottles from around the globe. It's a few blocks further west from Broadway, but worth the trek. Mostly bar snacks to complement the wine here. Join the Wine Club to extend the memory of the visit.

195 5 O'CLOCK SOMEWHERE BAR
AT: MARGARITAVILLE
RESORT TIMES SQUARE
560 7th Avenue,
32nd Fl.
(at W 40th St)
Times Square ⑥
+1 332 242 4826
*5oclocksomewhere
timessquare.com*

This is one of the kinder rooftop bars in the area, where you can relax and peer out over the excitement of Times Square and beyond. Drinks have a tropical bent here, in a nod to 'Margaritaville,' the hotel's name and theme. Bar snacks and dessert available. DJs on Friday and Saturday nights 7.30 to 11 pm.

FLIGHT CLUB

70 PLACES
TO SHOP

---

5 local bookshops for **BOOKWORMS** —————— 116

The 5 best **ART BOOK STORES** —————— 119

5 places to shop on a **GIRL'S TRIP** —————— 121

5 shops for those with **INDIVIDUAL STYLE** —— 123

5 **QUINTESSENTIALLY AMERICAN** shops
for everyone —————————————— 125

5 unique shops for **STREETWEAR** —————— 127

5 shops for the **FASHION FORWARD** ————— 129

5 **VINTAGE SHOPS** for the nostalgic collector— 132

5 shops for **FURNITURE**
and **HOME DECOR** ——————————— 134

5 specialty shops with **HISTORY** ————— 136

5 one-of-a-kind **GIFT** shops———————— 138

5 great **BEAUTY** shops ——————————— 140

5 stores for head-to-toe **ACCESSORIES** ——————— 142

5 **THEME STORES** for specific needs ——————— 144

5 local bookshops for
BOOKWORMS

---

196 ARGOSY BOOK STORE

116 East 59th St
(betw Lexington
and Park Ave)
Midtown East ⑥
+1 212 753 4455
argosybooks.com

As the oldest independent bookshop in New York City, it is in its third generation of family ownership. The shop occupies all seven floors of the building and they keep the shelves well-stocked with rare and out-of-print books, prints and maps. It might interest you to know that they are the founding members of the Antiquarian Booksellers Association and belong to the Appraisers Association of America.

197 THE STRAND

828 Broadway
(at E 12th St)
Greenwich Village ④
+1 212 473 1452
strandbooks.com

Advertised as 18 miles of books, they offer services unlike any other bookstore, and can curate a library to match both your personality *and* decor. Their special first editions are the ones that collectors drool over. It's an easy way to kill an afternoon, strolling the aisles or thumbing through the cheap books set up on the sidewalk outside.

199 **THREE LIVES & COMPANY**

198 GREENLIGHT

686 Fulton St
(at S Portland Ave)
Fort Greene,
Brooklyn ⑩
+1 718 246 0200
greenlightbookstore.com

Hooray for the independent bookseller. This forward-thinker was welcomed into the neighborhood with open arms. In-store events: on Saturday mornings kids get story time; evenings host more thoughtful conversations with leading authors. Some of their bigger book launches take place at BAM, and include the famous – like John Cleese, Elvis Costello, Lena Dunham, and Neil Gaiman.

199 THREE LIVES & COMPANY

154 West 10th St
(at Waverly Pl)
Greenwich Village ④
+1 212 741 2069
threelives.com

A cozy independent bookstore that's part of what makes the Village so quaint. On this corner since 1983, they are sure now to stay in the neighbourhood. Locals have learned to rely on owner Toby Cox's recommendations and come to the store regularly to share thoughts on books they have read.

200 MERCER STREET BOOKS

206 Mercer St
(betw W Houston
and Bleecker St)
West Village ④
+1 212 505 8615
mercerstreetbooks.com

This quaint bookshop is around the corner from the Angelika Film Center, shopping in Soho, Washington Square Park and the NYU campus. When the shop opened in 1990 it immediately attracted both writers and used booklovers. You will find it unpretentious and never lacking in interesting books or records. Small shops like these are disappearing, but your visit can help them stay open.

The 5 best
ART BOOK STORES

201 DASHWOOD BOOKS

33 Bond St
(betw Bowery and
Lafayette St)
Noho ④
+1 212 387 8520
dashwoodbooks.com

This charming Noho store – NYC's only independent bookstore devoted entirely to photography – is owned and operated by David Strettell, the former cultural director of Magnum Photos. Dashwood Books specializes in quality books on contemporary photography from the 1960s to the present, produced by outstanding publishers from Japan, Europe and the US. They also carry rare vintage books and numerous out-of-print and quality used titles.

202 MAST BOOKS

72 Avenue A
(at E 5th St)
East Village ④
+1 646 370 1114
mastbooks.com

Independently owned and one of New York's no-nonsense art book stores, Mast Books has a wonderful selection of out-of-print and secondhand books, periodicals, and rare editions. You'll find a great selection on fine art, photography, design, fashion and cinema, along with some literary fiction and poetry. They buy and sell, carry artists' catalogues, and new editions too.

203 URSUS

50 East 78th St
(betw Park and
Madison Ave)
Upper East Side ⑦
+1 212 772 8787
ursusbooks.com

You could get lost in this sanctum of art books, intriguing to collectors and beginning art lovers alike. Ursus is an institution with an unmatched collection of art books from five centuries, including the most rare illustrated books, catalogues and prints. Check the website to see the breadth and depth of their inventory.

204 192 BOOKS

192 10th Avenue
(at W 21st St)
Chelsea ⑤
+1 212 255 4022
www.192books.com

Operated by the Paula Cooper Gallery, known for its minimalist and conceptual art support, this store carries a well-curated selection of books on art and photography as well as literary fiction, history, and biography. They host readings, events and signing sessions, plus a weekly story hour for children on Wednesdays at 11 am.

205 ARTBOOK @ MOMA PS1

22-25 Jackson Ave
(at 46th Ave)
Long Island City,
Queens
+1 718 433 1088
artbook.com/
artbookps1

Founded by the people that run D.A.P, Artbook @ MoMA PS1 is a real museum bookstore that sells cutting-edge contemporary art books and magazines as well as catalogues, DVDs and CDs that you can't easily find elsewhere. There's a second, international magazine store in the museum lobby that carries more than 300 of the world's best magazines on art, fashion, design and culture.

5 places to shop on a
GIRL'S TRIP

---

206 NO.6

8 Centre Market Place
(betw Grand and
Broome St)
Little Italy ③
+1 212 226 5759
no6store.com

Stop here for a cool selection of clogs in spiffy colors and designs with both wedge and stacked heel (even in bootie styles), plus super-wearable pumps with splayed wide heels and slingbacks in pop colors. This shop was founded by Karin Bereson, a savvy vintage collector/stylist, so the clothes here are special too.

207 CLOAK & DAGGER

334 East 9th St
(betw 1st and 2nd Ave)
East Village ④
+1 212 673 0500
cloakanddagger
nyc.com

The uniqueness of this store lies in the 1960s cool-girl vibe and inviting mix of vintage and new. As a designer herself, the owner has a great eye and carries brands that reflect the store's aesthetic. Browsing is fun and employees are always well dressed, armed with smart style advice.

208 ARTISTS & FLEAS

AT: CHELSEA MARKET
88 10th Avenue
(at W 15th St)
Chelsea ⑤
+1 917 488 0044
artistsandfleas.com

This is a place to interact with artists and find little gems. Browse over 30 independent designers, foodie stalls and small eateries. The market holds a great range of goods by independent designers and shop owners ranging from art, music, vintage, handbags to handmade jewelry.

209 BERGDORF GOODMAN

754 5th Avenue
(betw 58th and
59th St)
Midtown ⑥
+1 212 753 7300
bergdorfgoodman.com

The landmark luxury department store you see today started out as a tailor shop in 1899 by Herman Bergdorf. If you have a healthy budget, here is where you can shop to your heart's content. We recommend going up to the seventh floor for afternoon tea and Central Park views. While it is not secret, it is sumptuous. The author of *Scatter My Ashes at Bergdorf Goodman* would agree.

210 NO RELATION VINTAGE

202 1st Avenue
(betw 12th and
13th St)
East Village ④
+1 212 228 5201
ltrainvintagenyc.com

No Relation Vintage belongs to the family of L Train Vintage shops. This is their only Manhattan location. Thrifting here with your friends is fun! If your travel agenda includes shopping for vintage jeans, T-shirts and jackets on a budget, this is the place to go. There are two floors of full racks giving you plenty of options.

5 shops for those with
INDIVIDUAL STYLE

211 **THE CAST**

72 Orchard St
(betw Grand and
Broome St)
Lower East Side ③
+1 212 228 2020
thecast.com

The Lower East Side punk rock scene might no longer exist, but thanks to those who continue to live the lifestyle and understand the aesthetic, you can still find a shop to help you look the part. The family-owned shop can help you customize a leather jacket, pick through the coolest vintage, and even assist you in discovering something for your child or pet. Rebellion has never looked so good.

212 **TRASH AND VAUDEVILLE**

96 East 7th St
(betw Ave A and
1st Ave)
East Village ④
+1 212 982 3590
trashandvaudeville.com

When downtown, make sure to stop by one of the last standing punk landmarks from the 1970s. The shop moved from its original location on St Marks Street to 7th Street, where it continues to uphold the institution and taste for all things punk and goth. The longtime store's manager, Jimmy Webb, passed in 2020 but remains an East Village legend.

213 LOVE ADORNED

269 Elizabeth St
(betw Prince and
Houston St)
Nolita ③
+1 888 920 5750
loveadorned.com

Fine and vintage jewelry collectors will appreciate this shop's one-of-a-kind inventory. Shopping here is a calm and inspiring experience. There are dry flowers, artisanal home decor products and, of course, jewelry. To further your experience, book yourself a piercing appointment. The prices can run a bit high, but consider it an investment..

214 PATRICIA FIELD ARTFASHION GALLERY

200 East Broadway,
Suite 3D
(betw Clinton and
Essex St)
Lower East Side ③
+1 212 966 4066
patriciafield.com

Sex and the City would never be the same without Patricia Field. The eccentric New Yorker and costume designer continues to be beloved by the fashion industry. Shop her signature looks in a gallery setting, which also highlights a hand-picked group of talented designers and visual artists. Fans of *Sex and the City* and *Emily in Paris*, this shop is a must-see in person.

215 FINE & DANDY

445 West 49th St
(betw 9th and
10th Ave)
Hell's Kitchen ⑥
+1 212 247 4847
fineanddandyshop.com

Spruce up your wardrobe with a custom shirt, pocket square, neckerchief, cufflinks or suspenders from the fine collection at this dapper gentleman's clothing store. The quaint shop belongs to the era of the well-dressed man about town. It is very cosmopolitan and you will walk out accessorized to the nines. Swell!

5 QUINTESSENTIALLY AMERICAN *shops for everyone*

216 **SCHOTT NYC**
236 Elizabeth St
(betw W Houston
and Prince St)
Nolita ③
+1 212 219 1636
schottnyc.com

Founded in 1913 by brothers Irving and Jack Schott, Schott continues the family tradition of manufacturing in the US. They are well known for the Perfecto motorcycle jacket, giving the Ramones their distinctive uniform, and Marlon Brando his tough look in *The Wild One*. Stop here for the latest and iconic styles in leather goods, bomber jackets and more. Near the Tenement Museum.

217 **FILSON**
876 Broadway
(betw 18th and
19th St)
Flatiron ⑤
+1 646 975 9855
filson.com

Filson represents the ruggedness of American heritage with quality outdoor essentials for all types of adventurers. Established in 1897, the Seattle-based outfitter and manufacturer has a reputation for reliability, style and excellent customer service. Shop this flagship location for durable clothing, accessories, knives and even utility belts. If it is good enough for loggers, sportsmen, miners, ranchers and the U.S. Forest Service, it is good enough for us.

218 DAVE'S NEW YORK

581 6th Avenue
(betw 16th and
17th St)
Chelsea ⑤
+1 212 989 6444
davesnewyork.com

One stop shop for All-American brands that withstand the test of time. Come here for durable, fire-resistant, and construction workwear, plus trendy items from brands like Levi's, Dickies, Carhartt. You might be surprised how popular these brands are with hip-hop artists and skateboarders.

219 REFORMATION

39 Bond St
(betw Bowery and
Lafayette St)
Noho ④
+1 646 603 0834
thereformation.com

Being naked is the number one sustainable option – after that, anything from Reformation. The brand is well known for their advocacy for sustainability in the fashion industry, and took the extra steps to build their own factory in Los Angeles. Step into the Bond Street location, for a shopping experience unlike any other. If this is your first purchase, their classic and stylish occasion dress should be your go-to.

220 SEARCH & DESTROY

25 St Marks Place
(betw 2nd and
3rd Ave)
East Village ④
+1 212 358 1120

A New York institution from the disappearing punk-rock scene. Go in with an open mind and nerves of steel because there is a lot to look through and it is not for the faint of heart. Their accessories will help you stand out from the mainstream crowd. Warning: some merchandise not suitable for children.

5 unique shops for
STREETWEAR

221 MR. THROWBACK

437 East 9th St
(betw 1st Ave and
Ave A)
East Village ④
+1 917 261 7834
mrthrowback.com

Vintage haven for sports enthusiasts. This nostalgic shop has 1980s and 1990s sports apparel, sneakers, video games and toys. Mr. Throwback started out at flea markets, making a name for himself as an expert in his field, and then set up shop in the East Village. Shop for original 90s Starter jackets, NBA Champion jerseys, Chalk Line jackets and other memorabilia.

222 KITH

337 Lafayette St
(betw Bleecker St
and Jones Alley)
Noho ④
+1 646 648 6285
kith.com

Sneaker connoisseurs from all over the world know to come here for the latest releases. This innovative brand has become a New York streetwear staple. They even have their own section at Bergdorf Goodman. The Soho shop is creatively designed and provides a unique shopping experience with milkshakes and ice cream. The whole family can take part because the multifunctional brand has men's, women's and kids' clothing.

223 ONLY NY

176 Stanton St
(betw Clinton and
Attorney St)
Lower East Side ③
+1 646 649 5673
onlyny.com

Shop like a New Yorker. This streetwear brand collaborates with city institutions like the MTA and *New York Magazine*. Only NY is where you shop if you want people to stop and ask, "Where did you get that?". In addition to teaming up with local artists and brands, the shop has its own widely recognized line that changes with each season.

224 SNEAK EZ

440 East 9th St
(betw 1st Ave and
Ave A)
East Village ④
+1 347 559 2513
sneakezshop.com

New York City streetwear designed by a real New Yorker. Sneak Ez consistently delivers with fun collaborations, an in-house line and now a coffee shop. The subtle designs and quality materials speak for themselves. Shop, grab a coffee and meet like-minded streetwear enthusiasts. Make sure to say hello to the mascot, MJ.

225 BILLIONAIRE BOYS CLUB

7 Mercer St
(betw Canal and
Grand St)
Soho ②
+1 212 777 2225
bbcicecream.com

From the moment you enter you just know this shop is as unique as Pharrel Williams himself. In 2003, the rapper and record producer teamed up with Japanese designer Nigo, and the two created a globally recognized lifestyle brand. Marrying streetwear and luxury, the shop carries an in-house line and brands like Comme des Garcons and Rizzoli books. Their focus is always on authenticity and culture.

5 *shops for the*
FASHION FORWARD

226 MARYAM NASSIR ZADEH

123 Norfolk St
(betw Delancey and
Rivington St)
Lower East Side ③
+1 212 673 6405
*maryamnassir
zadeh.com*

Maryam Nassir Zadeh, the shop's owner
and designer is known to New Yorkers
for her meticulous style that is reflected
in the store's selection. The shoes and
apparel are a minimalist's dream and
tailored to perfection for the office.
There is an aura of old-world chic and
fashion insiders flock here for Zadeh's
latest designs, plus a selection from
independent designers.

227 FIVESTORY

1020 Madison Avenue
(betw 78th and
79th St)
Upper East Side ⑦
+1 212 288 1338
fivestoryny.com

Luxury brand shoppers are always
seeking a unique experience and they can
find it on Madison Avenue. This concept
shop takes up an entire townhouse, and
feels like one big, but elegant, walk-in
closet. Roam the space and discover some
of your favorite designers. The carefully
curated selection makes shopping easy.
If you happen to like something in every
room, it means you have impeccable style.

228 THE REALREAL

80 Wooster St
(betw Broome and
Spring St)
Soho ②
+1 212 203 8386
therealreal.com

The RealReal has become online's number one consignment shop – and now you can soak it all up in person. New Yorkers see out convenience and designer bargains, The RealReal has all that and more, from dresses for hanging out to couture at half price. The store is oversized, beautiful, and well organized.

229 DOVER STREET MARKET

160 Lexington Avenue
(betw 30th and
31st St)
Murray Hill ⑥
+1 646 837 7750
doverstreetmarket.com

Fashion enthusiasts of unique and even one-of-a-kind items come here to spend money. You will be awed by the floors and floors of high-end designer goods. From top to bottom: the space, the clothes, the art installations and the staff are gorgeous and stylish. You will find many of your beloved brands under one roof here: Rick Owens, Supreme, Nike Lab... and a cafe to take a break from it all.

230 T.A.

332 West 13th St
(betw 14th St and
Gansevoort St)
Meatpacking
District ④
shop-ta.com

A modern concept shop that presents shoppers with unique and statement pieces and inspires younger generations to steer away from fast fashion. With many shops closing during the pandemic, Gen Z entrepreneur Telsha Anderson dreamed up the idea of a store where she personally edits indie brands from all over the world, like colorful Christopher John Rogers, feminine Rosie Assoulin and Maryam Nassir Zadeh.

5 VINTAGE SHOPS
for the nostalgic collector

---

231 COBBLESTONES

314 East 9th St
(betw 1st and 2nd Ave)
East Village ④
+1 212 673 5372
@cobblestonesvintagenyc

Step off the street and into a time capsule. This shop has been in the East Village since 1981 and is still going strong. Wardrobe stylists and celebrities enjoy shopping here because it is filled to the brim with vintage goodies. Make sure to really look around and try things on. The energetic owner has a distinctive style of her own and is always willing to help you find your perfect look.

232 9TH ST. VINTAGE

346 East 9th St
(betw 1st and 2nd Ave)
East Village ④
+1 917 265 8833
9thstvintage.com

Tucked away on Ninth Street is a special gem stocked with 1920s dresses, Levis, 1970s knits and even delicate lingerie. The interesting display window beckons you to come in and be a part of the nostalgia. Serious collectors and newbies alike come in to admire the owner's keen eye for one-of-a-kind treasures.

233 HAMLET'S VINTAGE

146 West 4th St
(betw MacDougal St
and 6th Ave)
Greenwich Village ④
+1 212 228 1561
hamletsvintage.com

From the 1940s to the 1990s, Hamlet's Vintage has something for everyone. With its blue awning and carefully arranged outdoor display the shop is hard to miss. The owner, Hamlet, is always present and happy to help you find the right style. Madonna has a shrine here and we hope one day she stops by to see it.

234 WHAT GOES AROUND COMES AROUND

351 West Broadway
(betw Grand and
Broome St)
Soho ②
+1 212 343 1225
whatgoesaround
nyc.com

In their own words, vintage is the new 'new'. This lifestyle shop is dedicated to fashion history. For investment-worthy vintage, like Chanel or Hermes, you have to make sure to stop by, it is a New York classic. They have the largest selection of high-end designer handbags and other noteworthy accessories from Prada, Versace, Fendi and Rolex. Investing in quality vintage is always a good idea.

235 NEW YORK VINTAGE

117 West 25th St
(betw 6th and 7th Ave)
Chelsea ⑤
+1 212 647 1107
newyorkvintage.com

No-nonsense vintage lovers and movie wardrobe stylists alike come here to shop for vintage couture. This shop has a lovely setup that will both charm you and inspire you. Vintage treasure hunters should expect to walk out with pricey but one-of-a-kind items that are too good to keep in the back of your closet.

5 shops for **FURNITURE** and **HOME DECOR**

236 PROPERTY

401 Broadway
(at Walker St)
Soho ②
+1 917 237 0123
propertyfurniture.com

Property's collections are always ahead of the curve and offer an eclectic mix you will not find anywhere else. Lighting, furniture and accessories wow, in a thoroughly modern style. Their showroom has tons of stuff, so go through it slowly, or you might miss something spectacular.

237 CREEL & GOW

131 East 70th St
(betw Madison and Park Ave)
Upper East Side ⑦
+1 212 327 4281
creelandgow.com

The cute Upper East Side shop carries some of the most rare and interesting luxury objects for home. Shopping here feels like browsing a small museum, with treasures from around the world. The entire collection is sourced by world travelers Jamie Creel, Marco Scarani, and their adventurous team. If you are a collector of curiosities this shop should be at the top of your list.

238 OLDE GOOD THINGS

333 West 52nd St
(betw 8th and 9th Ave)
Hell's Kitchen ⑥
+1 212 989 8814
ogtstore.com

A shop that feels like a romantic Parisian market. There are beautiful chandeliers, unusual antiques, and treasures pulled from historical places like the 1931 Waldorf Astoria Hotel and Towers. They specialize in architectural salvage and that is exactly what sets them apart from other antique stores. Shopping here will awaken your creative muse.

239 JOHN DERIAN COMPANY

6 East 2nd St
(betw Bowery and
2nd Ave)
East Village ④
+1 212 677 3917
johnderian.com

Here's a man with a style all his own, with a passion for decoupage. The style is eclectic Victorian with a sense of humor featuring whimsical animals, flora, seashells, butterflies, bugs and his signature eye. Each piece is handmade to order, with over 3000 designs to choose from. Also in store are the most magnificent candles made to look like pastries, and sweet recycled glass vases to complete the picture.

240 CURE THRIFT

91 3rd Avenue
(betw 12th and
13th St)
East Village ④
+1 212 505 7467
curethriftshop.com

A nonprofit thrift destination that recently moved to a more open and bright home. Owner and fourth-generation dumpster-diving New Yorker, Lizz Wolff, has a passion for sharing her love of everything vintage and obscure. Shop for furniture, clothing and help contribute to finding a cure for type 1 diabetes.

5 specialty shops with
HISTORY

241 C.O BIGELOW CHEMISTS

414 6th Avenue
(betw 8th and 9th St)
West Village ④
+1 212 533 2700
bigelowchemists.com

The oldest apothecary in America continues to do business in its original Greenwich Village location. This iconic pharmacy has whatever you might need in the personal care category. Unlike chain pharmacies this store has soft lighting, excellent customer service and their very own collection of products. Come in, buy the legendary hand salve, and be a part of history.

242 ECONOMY CANDY

108 Rivington St
(betw Ludlow and
Essex St)
Lower East Side ③
+1 212 254 1531
economycandy.com

A retro attraction that helps you satisfy that sweet tooth! This famous candy shop is stocked floor-to-ceiling with all of your childhood favorites, plus other candy you never even knew existed. Adults and kids alike cannot help but be impressed by the 2000-square-foot space where you can shop candy by the decade. Walk away with classics like the English butterscotch candy or imported Austrian Haribo gummies.

243 TANNEN'S MAGIC SHOP

45 West 34th St
(betw 5th and 6th Ave)
Midtown East ⑥
+1 212 929 4500
tannens.com

A mere three-minute walk from the Empire State Building is the oldest and most respected magic shop in the city. Founded by Louis Tannen in 1925, the hidden shop is a sight to see. The secret den is fun to find, and besides shopping for books and cards, you get to see an exhibit of Houdini relics. They put on intimate magic shows and the staff is beyond passionate about their craft.

244 MOOD FABRICS

225 West 37th St
(betw 7th and 8th Ave)
Garment District ⑥
+1 212 730 5003
moodfabrics.com

No one does fabric, buttons and trims like this popular fabric store. *Project Runway* might have made it famous, but fashion designers and students in the know have always flocked here for inspiration and fabrics by the yard. Open since the early 90s. Finding the exact location can be tricky, so make sure to take the elevator up to the third floor.

245 TOWN SHOP LINGERIE

2270 Broadway
(betw 81st and
82nd St)
Upper East Side ⑦
+1 212 595 6600
townshop.com

Voted the best lingerie store in the city, this shop has had a loyal following since 1888. You never need an appointment. Simply walk in, and walk out with the most comfortable bra of your life. They carry all types in sizes AA to K. The staff is very knowledgeable, and always kind and professional. While there, take a look in the swimwear department.

5 one-of-a-kind
G I F T shops

246 PINK OLIVE
439 East 9th St
(betw 1st Ave and
Ave A)
East Village ④
+1 212 780 0036
www.pinkolive.com

Escape into this magical shop for all your gift-giving needs. You will find artsy and smart greeting cards, art for your walls, baby gifts, home decor, candy, books. Bring your creative teen along. The service is a breath of fresh air, they honestly love helping you find what you need.

247 FISHS EDDY
889 Broadway
(betw 19th and
20th St)
Flatiron ⑤
+1 212 420 9020
fishseddy.com

When in Union Square take a detour to this quirky shop for all your kitchen needs. Their Statue of Liberty mugs look anything but basic. The eclectic selection includes dishes, flatware, tea towels, storage containers and vintage-style designs. The shop is beloved by New Yorkers and just celebrated their 35th anniversary. If you enjoy quality and funky designs this shop will make you smile.

248 NILU GIFT SHOP

191 Malcolm X Blvd
(betw 119th and
120th St)
Harlem ⑧
+1 646 964 4926
shopnilu.com

Explore Harlem's rich history with a walking tour, then shop for gifts at NiLu. The brilliant owner created an online lifestyle brand and a brick-and-mortar destination that the whole community enjoys. The shop beautifully displays scented candles, pillows, personal care items and books. NiLu features Black authors, makers and local artists. If you're looking for gifts for kids, stop by Grandma's Place around the corner.

249 MOMA DESIGN STORE

44 West 53rd St
(betw 5th and 6th Ave)
Midtown ⑥
+1 212 767 1050
store.moma.org

Take a short walk from the Radio City Music Hall or the MoMA Museum itself and shop for quirky and design-y gifts. This is not your typical gift shop. The enticing selection of cutting-edge design products is made exclusively for the museum. No matter your taste, you will surely find something to help you keep the memory of your visit alive.

250 EXIT9 GIFT EMPORIUM

AT: AGELOFF TOWERS
51 Avenue A
(betw 3rd and 4th St)
East Village ④
+1 212 228 0145
shopexit9.com

Ask any East Village local where to shop for gifts and they will point you to this mom-and-pop shop. The eclectic selection reflects the vibrancy of the neighborhood. They go above and beyond to assist you to select souvenirs, goodie bags, and curated gift boxes. They are a certified LGBT business from the National Gay and Lesbian Chamber of Commerce. Another good reason to support them!

5 great
B E A U T Y shops

---

251 BITE BEAUTY LIP LAB
174 Prince St
(betw Sullivan and
Thompson St)
Soho ②
+1 646 484 6111
bitebeauty.com

The brainy creators of Bite have set up a lab for anyone who enjoys a good tube of lipstick. Beauty addicts and those who struggle to find their perfect match come here to find beauty bliss. The space is welcoming and creative, mirroring a bakery environment. So witty! Go find your personal shade of red lipstick.

252 FUEGUIA 1833
21 Crosby St
(betw Howard and
Grand St)
Soho ②
+1 646 692 3051
fueguia.com

Upscale perfumery shop with a stunning interior. This is an excellent place to find your new scent with the help of a knowledgeable staff. The sustainable brand allows you to experience exotic botanicals from Patagonia. The sensory therapy will have you coming back for more.

253 KIEHL'S SINCE 1851

109 3rd Avenue
(betw 13th and
14th St)
East Village ④
+1 212 677 3171
kiehls.com

The brand might be a chain, but this shop is the original. Kiehl's was founded more than 170 years ago at this exact location. If you find yourself in the neighborhood, make sure to stop by for this old-world apothecary and experience the charm, friendly service, and effective products with expert help from devoted staff.

254 ALLURE STORE

191 Lafayette St
(betw Broome and
Grand St)
Lower East Side ③
+1 855 917 4127
allure.shop

You can now shop beauty products right out of the pages of your favorite magazine. Curated by beauty editors, this store highlights the best in skincare and makeup. The stylish interior and soothing colors elevate the experience. There are over 150 brands to choose from, and you'll have the opportunity to try them out in person.

255 AEDES PERFUMERY

16-A Orchard St
(betw Canal and
Hester St)
Lower East Side ③
+1 212 206 8674
aedes.com

A swanky perfumery and beauty shop unlike any other. From French perfumes to high-end candles, every product they sell has a special story and can be a beautiful gift. The ritzy beauty destination allows you to sample products that you will never find in a mainstream shop.

5 stores for head-to-toe
ACCESSORIES

___

256 JJ HAT CENTER

310 5th Avenue
(betw W 31st
and 32nd St)
Midtown ⑥
+1 212 239 4368
jjhatcenter.com

Introduce something classic and swanky into your life. This hat shop is the oldest in New York, boasting a space and set of loyal customers epitomizing a world of class. Service is top notch, everyone working here is a pro, so you and your hat will be taken care of for life, including steaming and shaping.

257 FABULOUS FANNY'S

335 East 9th St
(betw 1st and 2nd Ave)
East Village ④
+1 212 533 0637
fabulousfannys.com

If you have to wear glasses, be different. Whether your preferred style of frame is classic or spiffy, Fabulous Fanny's is like a mini capsule of styles from different eras. Movie sets rely on them for their collection of frames that go back to the 1700s. A dying breed in New York, you would be wise to go experience it.

258 THE GREAT FROG

72 Orchard St
(betw Broome and
Grand St)
Lower East Side ③
+1 646 370 5727
*thegreatfrog
london.com*

Rock 'n' roll jewelry created for anyone who considers themselves an outsider. The distinctive style of their silver jewelry is rooted in British punk culture, and continues to be owned by the family that founded it in 1972. Their clients are some of the biggest names in Hollywood and the music industry. A great place to come and get acquainted with their one-of-a-kind selection.

259 FLIGHT CLUB

812 Broadway
(at West 11th St)
Greenwich Village ④
flightclub.com

More for the fashion crowd than serious runners. Serious fanatics and collectors can search through walls and walls of name-brand sneakers: new, vintage and lusted-after. Consignment rules, so sizes are random, upping the thrill of the hunt. Opposite the sneakers is a wall of baseball caps, so you can coordinate your purchase.

260 EAST VILLAGE HATS

80 East 7th St
(betw 1st and 2nd Ave)
East Village ④
+1 212 358 7092
eastvillagehats.nyc

From bowlers to wedding hats, the expert proprietor of this shop can handcraft or sell you the hat of your dreams. Entering the millinery shop helps you time travel and imagine yourself wearing art from another century. You can tell each hat on display was made with love and care. Visit them on any occasion you require a hat to complete your look.

5 THEME STORES
for specific needs

---

261 SATURDAYS NYC
SURFING

31 Crosby St
(betw Grand and
Broome St)
Soho ②
+1 347 449 1668
saturdaysnyc.com

For those into riding waves, get a fix of surf life here. Start with a signature blend espresso, browse surfboards, men's attire, books, then make your way to the backyard — where you might meet fellow surfers and swap tales. The style is laidback, with a bent for cotton and natural fabrics in soft colors.

262 PRINTED MATTER
INDIE PRINTS

231 11th Avenue
(at 26th St)
Chelsea ⑤
+1 212 925 0325
printedmatter.org

Founded by Sol LeWitt and several other artists, this nonprofit bookstore specializes in serious and political artists' books, zines, posters, and prints, including an extensive selection of out-of-print material. Their goal is to preserve and provide insight into publications made and distributed by artists. Ongoing events include zine releases, exhibitions, and book announcements.

263 SPARK PRETTY
1990S

333 East 9th St
(betw 1st and 2nd Ave)
East Village ④
+1 646 850 0327
sparkpretty.com

Nineties kids will be over the moon shopping here, reminiscing about their favorite decade. The owner, Amanda Dolan, worked as a stylist with Betsey Johnson and has an excellent eye. The shop has been known to have a celebrity or two stop in and enjoy the fun aesthetic. Shop for custom jeans jackets, accessories, and toys, like the troll dolls.

264 ERGOT RECORDS
VINYL

32 East 2nd St
(betw Bowery St and 2nd Ave)
East Village ④
+1 312 351 3232
ergotrecords.
blogspot.com

With younger generations appreciating vinyl records it only makes sense that artist and label owner, Adrian Rew, ventured into retail. The community-friendly space holds small performances, readings, and DJ sets. The selection is never lacking in diversity, ranging from jazz, salsa, punk, disco, hip-hop, house and experimental. Unlike a lot of other vinyl shops, this relaxing space is minimal and invites a conversation.

265 AN.MÉ /AHN-MAY/
COOL KIDS

249 Bleecker St
(betw Ave of the Americas and Bedford St)
West Village ④
+1 646 719 1116
anmeshop.com

A female-owned independent boutique that makes shopping for kid's clothing and accessories easy. From newborns to pre-teens, this shop has the coolest selection of stylish products from all over the world. The shop inspires imagination with products like Russian Roly Poly, Sonny Angel action figures, Monchhichi dolls and more. The adorable selection is always changing and aims to please the pickiest of kids.

FLATIRON BUILDING

25 BUILDINGS TO ADMIRE

5 *buildings with* **HISTORY** ——————————— 148

5 *impressive* **EARLY SKYSCRAPERS** ————— 150

5 *must-see* **MODERN** *buildings* ——————————— 152

5 *places to* **ADMIRE THE VIEW** ——————— 154

5 *incredible* **PLACES OF WORSHIP** ————— 156

5 buildings with
HISTORY

266 **ANGEL ORENSANZ FOUNDATION**
172 Norfolk St
Lower East Side ③
+1 212 253 0452
orensanz.org

This art and performance space, located in a neo-Gothic structure in the Lower East Side, is the oldest surviving synagogue in New York City (from 1849). It fell into disrepair after World War II, but the Jewish Spanish sculptor and painter Angel Orensanz restored it in 1986. Now it serves as the artist's studio and a center for the arts.

267 FRAUNCES TAVERN

267 FRAUNCES TAVERN

54 Pearl St
(at Broad St)
Financial District ①
+1 212 425 1778
*frauncestavern
museum.org*

This landmarked 1719 building was HQ to George Washington during the American Revolution. Originally built by Henry Holt, who taught dance and held balls in the space. Take a guided tour to be taken back to colonial times. Or, take in history at the still operating tavern.

268 LIBRARY OF BRONX COMMUNITY COLLEGE

2155 University
Avenue
The Bronx
+1 718 289 5100
bcc.cuny.edu

A beautiful example of a Beaux Arts building designed by architect Stanford White, featuring the breathtaking dome of the Gould Memorial Library, outfitted in marble, mosaics, and Tiffany glass. At its rear, The Hall of Fame offers views of the Harlem River and busts of great Americans.

269 TRINITY CHURCH

75 Broadway
(at Wall St)
Financial District ①
+1 212 602 0800
trinitywallstreet.org

It's amusing to think that Trinity Church was once the tallest structure in NYC. Its Gothic Revival architecture dates back to 1846, with surrounding cemetery dating back much further, housing the grave of Alexander Hamilton, America's first Secretary of the Treasury (and current Broadway musical smash). Concerts are held regularly in St. Paul's Chapel.

270 GRAND CENTRAL STATION

89 East 42nd St
(at Park Ave)
Midtown ⑥
+1 212 340 2583
*grandcentral
terminal.com*

Opened in 1913, the main train hub in NYC harkens back to a time of sophisticated travel. Meet at the Clock, which is centered below the Sky Ceiling, an opulent astronomical mural. Downstairs, in front of the Oyster Bar, is the famous whisper wall, from which two people can communicate via whisper from opposite archways.

5 impressive
EARLY SKYSCRAPERS

271 **CHRYSLER BUILDING**
405 Lexington Avenue
(at E 42nd St)
Midtown ⑥
chryslerbuilding.com

New York's most adored skyscraper, because of its elegant and sublime art deco detailing, inside and out. Famous for its stylized eagles at the corners of its arched crown (even prettier at night). Gargoyles match the medieval ones on Paris' Notre Dame. Pop into the lobby to admire its luxe mix of marble, and the ceiling mural.

272 **WOOLWORTH BUILDING**
233 Broadway
(betw Barclay St
and Park Pl)
Financial District ①
+1 203 966 9663
woolworthtours.com

Our personal favorite because of its ornate façade, a resemblance to many European Gothic cathedrals. The building was commissioned by F.W. Woolworth, owner of the famous five-and-dime chain, and designed by architect Cass Gilbert in 1913. To get inside, sign up for a tour or head to the restaurant, The Wooly Public.

273 FLATIRON BUILDING

175 5th Avenue
(at E 23rd St)
Flatiron ⑤

Named the Flatiron, due to its shape resembling a clothes iron, the wedge-shaped steel-framed building was completed in 1902. Residents were skeptical that the building could remain standing, considering its width of only 6 ½ feet (1,95 meters) at its narrowest point. Adjacent to Madison Square Park.

274 ROCKEFELLER CENTER

45 Rockefeller Plaza
Midtown ⑥
+1 212 332 6868
rockefellercenter.com

Nineteen art deco-style buildings, whose main building, '30 Rock', houses NBC studios. Walk by in the early morning to witness the scene of *Today Show* fans vying to get on the air. For views, head to The Observation Deck or the bar in the Rainbow Room. Winter brings the annual Christmas tree and ice skating rink.

275 WILLIAMSBURGH SAVINGS BANK TOWER

1 Hanson Place
(at Flatbush Ave)
Downtown
Brooklyn ⑪

Brooklyn's high point is often referred to as its 'most phallic building'. The four-sided clock tower was a bank but is now a luxury condo. The ground floor still retains the vaulted bank hall as an event space, and the winter home to the Brooklyn Flea which sells vintage clothing, collectibles, and crafts by local designers.

5 must-see
MODERN *buildings*

---

276 **WORLD TRADE CENTER OCULUS**

Church St
(betw Dey
and Fulton St)
Financial District ①
*officialworldtrade
center.com*

Part of the World Trade Center Development, this stunning structure by Santiago Calatrava is a breathtaking achievement designed to symbolize the light that can still shine after the darkness of tragedy. This is a hub of the PATH train station and also has a gorgeous shopping mall. Don't miss the tunnel to the Winter Garden.

277 **NEW YORK BY GEHRY**

8 Spruce St
(betw Nassau
and William St)
Financial District ①
+1 212 877 2220
newyorkbygehry.com

World-renowned architect Frank Gehry's eye-catching undulating tower. It stands next to the iconic Woolworth Building and at 76 stories it's one of tallest residential skyscrapers in the world. Clad in stainless steel it catches the light and its curves allow windows to project for unparalleled views.

278 **VIA 57 WEST**

625 West 57th St
(betw 11th Ave
and West Side Hwy)
Hell's Kitchen ⑥
+1 646 630 7917
via57west.com

On the Hudson River sits a dramatic pyramid, with a trapezoid cut-out housing a courtyard with trees, a totally new example of residential living in NYC. Architect Bjarke Ingels incorporated many eco-conscious ideas into his design. Best viewed from one of the city's tour boats.

279 56 LEONARD

56 Leonard St
(betw Church St
and W Broadway)
Tribeca ③
+1 212 965 1500
56leonardtribeca.com

Tribeca's tallest residential tower, designed by the Swiss architecture firm Herzog & De Meuron, is a wonder seen from anywhere in the neighborhood. New Yorkers often refer to it as the 'Jenga Building' due to its stacked cantilevered design. Artist Anish Kapoor's bean sculpture, which appears to be holding up the building at ground level, coming soon.

280 ONE57

157 West 57th St
Midtown ⑥
+1 212 570 1700
one57.com

This striking 1005-foot-tall glass tower is a good example of the building frenzy along 57th Street, making this the new upscale residential stretch. It's marketed as 'above and beyond' because of its views over Central Park, and it's also one of the buildings that ignited a very New York-ish discussion over loss of sunlight over the southern part of the park.

280 ONE57

5 places to
ADMIRE THE VIEW

---

281 TOP OF THE ROCK
AT: ROCKEFELLER CENTER
30 Rockefeller Plaza
(entrance on W 50th St)
Midtown ⑥
+1 877 692 7625
topoftherocknyc.com

For a more intimate, nestled view of the city, head to the tri-level observatory deck on top of Rockefeller Center. Featuring areas indoors and out, this spot reveals the building's art deco touches. Learn the history of the area as you ascend and be sure to look up while you're in the elevator.

282 ONE WORLD TRADE CENTER
285 Fulton St
(at West St)
Financial District ①
+1 844 696 1776
oneworld observatory.com

Go 104 floors to reach the top of the tallest skyscraper in the Western hemisphere where you'll get panoramic views – as long as it's not cloudy. On the way up, elevators clad in high res screens will show you how NYC went from fields to a small village to the metropolis it is today. Buy tickets online to save time.

283 BELVEDERE CASTLE
AT: CENTRAL PARK
Mid-Park at 79th St
Central Park ⑦
+1 212 772 0288
centralparknyc.org

For views of a more bucolic nature, position yourself inside the middle of Central Park. This castle has two balconies providing views of the reservoir, the south lawns and beyond. You can borrow binoculars from the nature observatory located inside the castle.

284 SUMMIT ONE VANDERBILT

45 East 42nd St
Midtown East ⑥
+1 877 682 1401
summitov.com

A real tourist attraction but seeing Manhattan from this high up, especially at dawn or nightfall, is pretty spectacular. This immersive art installation with 25.000 square feet of mirrors designed by Kenzo Digital is fun and boasts tremendous views of the Manhattan skyline. Don't miss *Clouds* by the Japanese artist Yayoi Kusama before heading to the observation deck and the external glass elevator.

285 1 HOTEL BROOKLYN BRIDGE

60 Furman St
(betw Doughty St and
Brooklyn Bridge Park)
Brooklyn Heights ⑩
+1 347 696 2500
1hotels.com

With a view of the Brooklyn Bridge, Manhattan Bridge, and Statue of Liberty, you've hit the downtown triple trifecta. On the roof you can also admire the L-shaped lap pool from the huge veranda. Great spot if you like being by the water with lots to do on both sides.

282 ONE WORLD TRADE CENTER

5 incredible
PLACES OF WORSHIP

286 ELDRIDGE STREET SYNAGOGUE

12 Eldridge St
(betw Canal and
Division St)
Lower East Side ③
+1 212 219 0302
eldridgestreet.org

East European immigrants built this synagogue in 1887, one of the first in the US. Jewish numerology can be spotted: 12 rondels for the 12 tribes of Israel, 5 arches representing Books of Moses, and 4 wooden doors for the 4 matriarchs. Important Jewish families once frequented this beautiful space with soaring 70-foot ceilings and stained glass. Now a museum.

287 RIVERSIDE CHURCH

490 Riverside Drive
(at W 120th St)
Harlem ⑧
+1 212 870 6700
trcnyc.org

This church is famed for its Neo-Gothic architecture but even more so for its place in the fight for social justice. Martin Luther King Jr. spoke here against the Vietnam War. Cesar Chavez and Nelson Mandela visited it, as well as theological 'superstar' Reinhold Niebuhr. Boasts the largest *carillon* (bell tower).

288 ST MARK'S CHURCH-IN-THE-BOWERY

131 East 10th St
(at 2nd Ave)
East Village ④
+1 212 674 6377
stmarksbowery.org

The oldest site of continuous worship in Manhattan is still a progressive force honoring diversity and civil rights. Andy Warhol screened his early movies here. The Poetry Project, which many famous poets have read at, including Allen Ginsberg and Patti Smith, is still active today. Ongoing events include mindful meditation and discussions.

289 CATHEDRAL CHURCH OF ST JOHN THE DIVINE

1047 Amsterdam Ave
(at W 112th St)
Morningside
Heights ⑧
+1 212 316 7540
stjohndivine.org

World's largest cathedral, built by Freemasons, is a mecca of hidden symbolism carved into columns and sculpture, including references to its namesake, who had a vision of the end of the world. Annual rituals include The Blessing of the Animals, Procession of the Ghouls, The Blessing of the Bicycles, and a Winter Solstice Celebration.

290 CHURCH OF THE TRANSFIGURATION

"LITTLE CHURCH
AROUND THE CORNER"
1 East 29th St
(betw 5th and
Madison Ave)
Nomad ⑤
+1 212 684 6770
littlechurch.org

Founded in 1848 to embrace all races, classes and sexual orientations, this early English Neo-Gothic style features a quaint English-style garden in front. Also known as the 'wedding church'. The complex includes eclectic side chapels and a 14th-century stained glass window. Free concerts in the main church.

VIEW FROM BROOKLYN BRIDGE PARK

75 PLACES
TO DISCOVER
NEW YORK

5 monuments to **GREAT MEN** and **WOMEN** —— 162

The 5 most impressive **MEMORIALS** ————— 164

5 **HISTORIC HOUSES**
that fire the imagination ————————— 166

5 public library **READING ROOMS** ————— 168

5 **CITY PARKS** to revel in ——————— 172

5 **CENTRAL PARK** attractions ————— 175

5 great neighborhood **WALKS** ————— 177

5 historic places in **BROOKLYN HEIGHTS** —— 180

5 must-see **SPORTS** ——————— 182

5 ways to **SIGHTSEE** via public transport ——— 184

5 cool ways to **MINGLE** with New Yorkers ——— 186

5 ways to enjoy **NYC FROM THE WATER** —— 188

The 5 best ways to get **PHYSICAL** ——————— 190

5 eras to witness **NYC** *in*
BOOKS *and* **MOVIES** ————————— 192

5 things that **NEW YORKERS** *just* **KNOW** —— 194

5 monuments to
GREAT MEN and WOMEN

291 **FEARLESS GIRL STATUE**

Broad St
(betw Wall St
and Exchange Pl)
Financial District ①

New York has fallen in love with this delightfully valiant little girl. The bronze sculpture by Kristen Visbal depicts a defiant lass – who once stood facing the bull of Wall Street. The statue initially appeared on International Women's Day to symbolize female empowerment. It now has its permanent spot in front of the New York Stock Exchange.

292 **MARQUIS DE LAFAYETTE**

Park Avenue South
(at E 16th St and east
end of Union Square)
Union Square ⑤

This French nobleman came to the aid of the colonies in their fight against the British during the Revolutionary War. The statue was designed by Frédéric-Auguste Bartholdi (who also designed the Statue of Liberty) and is a token of appreciation from the French government for aid provided during the Franco-Prussian War.

293 ABRAHAM LINCOLN

Union Square Park
(north end of Park,
at E 16th St)
Union Square ⑤

Cast in 1870, this larger-than-life bronze of Honest Abe looks south over the green quadrant of Union Square and the equestrian George Washington on the square's south end, both by sculptor Henry Kirke Brown. Controversy erupted when the statue was unveiled, due to the fact that Lincoln wore a toga over his suit.

294 FIORELLO LA GUARDIA

LaGuardia Place
(at Bleecker St)
Greenwich Village ④
nycgovparks.org

Upbeat statue of the 99th mayor of New York City, who served for three terms from 1934 to 1945. The famous New Deal Democrat was successful in linking national money with local needs. He was born in Greenwich Village, and was only 5,2 feet tall (1,57 meters) – hence his nickname, the 'Little Flower' (*fiorello* in Italian).

295 HARRIET TUBMAN

Harriet Tubman
Memorial Plaza
(W 122nd St,
St Nicholas Avenue
and Frederick
Douglass Blvd)
Harlem ⑧
nycgovparks.org

Renowned American abolitionist. Born a slave, she escaped and helped numerous other slaves escape the South through the use of the so-called 'underground railroad'. Her dress depicts faces of slaves and some of the items they might have carried. Along the base are tiles that mimic quilt patterns with folk traditions.

The 5 most impressive
MEMORIALS

296 **FRANKLIN D. ROOSEVELT FOUR FREEDOMS PARK**
1 FDR Four Freedoms Park (southern tip of Roosevelt Island) Roosevelt Island +1 212 204 8831 *fdrfourfreedoms park.org*

Located on the narrow island in the East River between Manhattan and Queens, this memorial is dedicated to FDR's four freedoms which he espoused in his 1941 State of the Union Address: freedom of speech and expression, freedom of worship, freedom from want and freedom from fear. Take the Roosevelt Island Tramway to get there, which adds extra drama.

297 **IRISH HUNGER MEMORIAL**
North End Ave and Vesey St Battery Park City ① +1 212 267 9799 *bpca.ny.gov*

Overlooking the Hudson river, an elevated grassy hill represents the Ireland so many immigrants left behind to build a future in New York, as a result of the Great Irish Famine (1845-1852). The hill contains stones from each of Ireland's 32 counties. Tip: grab a coffee in the small bar on the corner.

298 GRANT'S TOMB

Riverside Drive
(at W 122nd St)
Harlem ⑧
+1 212 666 1640
www.nps.gov

The largest mausoleum in North America is that of Union Army general Ulysses S. Grant, who successfully defeated the Confederacy during the Civil War and went on to become the 18th president. Grant insisted on this location so his wife could be buried by his side.

299 AFRICAN BURIAL GROUND MEMORIAL

AT: TED WEISS
FEDERAL BUILDING
290 Broadway
(betw Duane
and Reade St)
Financial District ①
+1 212 637 2019
www.nps.gov/afbg

This recently discovered burial site contains the remains of 15.000 both free and enslaved Africans who lived in Manhattan from the late 1600s until 1794. The outdoor memorial was designed by Rodney Leon, and sits next to an exhibition space detailing the African contribution to the building of early New York City.

300 MUSEUM OF JEWISH HERITAGE

A LIVING MEMORIAL
TO THE HOLOCAUST
36 Battery Place
(inside Battery Park
near 1st Pl)
Battery Park City ①
+1 646 437 4202
mjhnyc.org

On the edge of the Hudson River lies a symbolic six-sided building with a pyramid roof, alluding to the 6 points of the Jewish star and the six million Jews who died during the Holocaust. Inside, a permanent exhibition utilizes personal accounts and artifacts of survivors. Check the calendar for other special exhibitions.

5 HISTORIC HOUSES
that fire the imagination

301 **MORRIS-JUMEL MANSION**
AT: ROGER MORRIS PARK
65 Jumel Terrace
(betw W 160th
and 162nd St)
Washington
Heights ⑧
+1 212 923 8008
morrisjumel.org

Manhattan's oldest house has had many illustrious dwellers. Built in 1765 as a country estate it also served as HQ for George Washington, was the home of Aaron Burr, and the outrageous and illegitimate daughter of a Rhode Island prostitute Eliza Bowen Jumel who became mistress of the house. Tour the house itself and current exhibition.

302 **GRACIE MANSION**
East End Avenue
(at E 88th St)
Upper East Side ⑦
+1 212 676 3060
graciemansion.org

Since 1942, Gracie Mansion, one of the oldest surviving wood structures in Manhattan, has been home to the mayors of New York City and their families. The two-story mansion overlooks a sleepy, scenic bend of the East River in Carl Schurz Park. Its main two floors are open to the public on a limited basis for guided tours and serve as a small museum.

303 THEODORE ROOSEVELT BIRTHPLACE

28 East 20th St
(betw Park Ave
and Broadway)
Flatiron ⑤
+1 212 260 1616
nps.gov/thrb

The 26th president of the United States was born in a quaint townhouse. This museum is a replica of the original house rebuilt in 1919 and showcases many interesting objects from his time, like his Rough Rider uniform, his favorite chair, and an eyeglass case with bullet hole from an assassination attempt.

304 DYCKMAN FARMHOUSE MUSEUM

4881 Broadway
(at W 204th St)
Inwood ⑧
+1 212 304 9422
dyckmanfarmhouse.org

The oldest surviving farmhouse on the island of Manhattan is a throw-back to the city's agrarian past. Built in Dutch colonial style around 1780 by William Dyckman, his family farmed the land well into the 19th century. Artifacts include family objects and archaeological objects from surrounding grounds, like cannon balls from the American Revolution.

305 THE MORGAN LIBRARY & MUSEUM

225 Madison Avenue
(at E 36th St)
Midtown ⑥
+1 212 685 0008
themorgan.org

Originally built to house the library of John Pierpont Morgan, financier and banker extraordinaire, presently a museum that holds his art collection – among other treasures. Peter Paul Rubens' drawings and the manuscript of Mozart's Haffner symphony are here. Architect Renzo Piano added a controversial, modern entrance to the library in 2006, his first project in New York.

5 public library
READING ROOMS

306 **ROSE MAIN READING ROOM**
AT: NEW YORK PUBLIC LIBRARY
476 5th Avenue (at E 42nd St)
Midtown ⑥
+1 917 275 6975
nypl.org

This cathedral-like reading room is a true treasure, on par with the library Sainte-Geneviève in Paris. Newly restored to the tune of 12 million dollars, the impressive plaster ceiling – decorated with paintings of the sky, and gilded rosettes – has been reborn. The century-old Beaux-Arts room is two city blocks long, with 42 communal tables, and 52-foot ceilings.

307 **BROOKLYN PUBLIC LIBRARY**
FOR NEW YORKERS: CENTRAL LIBRARY
10 Grand Army Plaza (at Flatbush Ave and Eastern Parkway)
Prospect Heights, Brooklyn ⑪
+1 718 230 2100
bklynlibrary.org

On the edge of Prospect Park sits a majestic, curved, art deco building highlighted by a jaw-dropping 50-foot entryway decked by two massive walls adorned with stylized gold-leaf figures. Fifteen bronze panels here celebrate icons of American literature – Edgar Allen Poe's *The Raven*, Mark Twain's *Tom Sawyer* and a whale for Herman Melville's *Moby Dick*.

308 THE EXPLORERS CLUB

46 East 70th St
(betw Park and
Madison Ave)
Upper East Side ⑦
+1 212 628 8383
explorers.org

To gain access to this library you have to make an appointment with this private club's curator Lacey Flint, but the beauty of what you'll find is more than worth that small effort. You'll be impressed by the 5000-volume map collection, and Thor Heyerdahl's Kon-Tiki globe. The 1910 Jacobean mansion is filled with an assortment of taxidermy and other global travel souvenirs.

309 THE NEW YORK SOCIETY LIBRARY

53 East 79th St
(betw Madison and
Park Ave)
Upper East Side ⑦
+1 212 288 6900
nysoclib.org

This five-story Italianate townhouse houses the oldest library in the city full of rare and exquisite books, founded in 1754. It functioned as the Library of Congress during New York's brief reign as America's capitol. It it supported by its members, but the first floor reading room and exhibits are open to all.

310 THE GENERAL SOCIETY OF MECHANICS AND TRADESMEN LIBRARY

20 West 44th St
(betw 5th and 6th Ave)
Midtown ⑥
+1 212 840 1840
generalsociety.org

Contains more than 100.000 volumes including books on various trades – carpenters, blacksmiths, plumbers – that have made up its membership. The main reading room's magnificent space is highlighted by an enormous copper-and-wrought-iron skylight, and three stories of balconies surrounding it, one of which holds its collection of clever locks, one dating back to Egypt BC.

5 CITY PARKS

to revel in

311 THE HIGH LINE

From Gansevoort
and Washington St
to W 34th St &
12th Avenue
Multiple entrances
along 10th Avenue
Chelsea ⑤
thehighline.org

A disused rail line from the 1930s has been transformed into a 1,5-mile-long landscaped wonderland, perched 30 ft above the street. An exciting new breed of modern building has taken over the area too – the HL 23, the crooked building on 23rd and the IAC Building, the frosted, amorphic giant between 18th and 19th Streets. Start your walk at the Whitney Museum.

312 DOMINO PARK

River St
(betw S 5th and
Grand St)
Williamsburg,
Brooklyn ⑨
dominopark.com

Another fine spot along the East River, this park sits in front of the city's landmarked Domino Sugar Refinery, once a force in the neighborhood's economy, now an office building. The 6-acre park has a wonderful promenade, which incorporates salvaged equipment from the refinery as sculptures and delightfully transformed into a colorful children's playground.

313 INWOOD HILL PARK

Dyckman St
(at Payson Ave)
Inwood ⑧
nycgovparks.org

At the northwestern tip of Manhattan is 196 acres overlooking the Bronx, where you can also see two bridges spanning the East River, and a serene section of the Hudson. The natural forest, valleys and ridges hold remnants of the ancient and even prehistoric New York when the Lenape Native American tribes used the caves as dwellings.

314 LITTLE ISLAND

AT: PIER 55
Meatpacking
District ④
littleisland.org

This charming little island on the edge of the Meatpacking District in the Hudson River is worth a visit for the design by Thomas Heatherwick and for its beautiful trees, flowers and grasses. There's a 687-seat amphitheater and stunning views of the city as well as the Hudson River and New Jersey.

315 GREEN-WOOD CEMETERY

500 25th St
(at 5th Ave)
Brooklyn ⑪
+1 718 768 7300
green-wood.com

Founded in 1838 as one of the first rural cemeteries in America. Their 478 acres are donned with beautiful statuary and mausoleums, and a stunning entry gate. Check the calendar for events, like the annual tour of the catacombs. Famous folks buried here: artist Jean-Michel Basquiat, Leonard Bernstein, Frank Morgan – the wiz of *The Wizard of Oz*.

5 CENTRAL PARK

attractions

from Central Park West to 5th Avenue
Central Park N to W 59th St
Central Park ⑦
+1 212 310 6600
www.centralparknyc.org

316 CONSERVATORY GARDEN
Betw 5th Avenue
and E 105th St

A less traveled, more formal part of the park. Its six acres hold a special assortment of English, French and Italian flowers and is set up as a quiet zone, creating one of the more calm spots in Manhattan. Enter through the wrought iron Vanderbilt Gate, once the entry to a Vanderbilt estate before it was donated to the city.

317 MALL AND LITERARY WALK
On the east side of
the park, from
E 67th to 69th St

This grand promenade is the only straight path in Central Park, framed by beautiful American elm trees. Start at Center Drive, stroll past the Naumburg Bandshell to the Bethesda Terrace. At the southern end of the mall you can admire some sculptures. You may remember seeing the promenade in the movies *Kramer vs. Kramer* and *Maid in Manhattan*.

318 **LAMP POST GPS**

Lost? Use lamp posts to pinpoint where you are in the park. A small placard with four numbers is attached to each lamp post. The first two numbers represent the street, the second two numbers indicate if you are on the east or west side – even is east, odd is west.

319 **NORTH WOODS**

West side to mid park from W 101st to 110th St

The biggest of the three woodlands in the upper part of the park was designed to have a natural, wild look, with streams and archways leading to the peaceful Ravine at its heart. Walk through Loch's Tunnel, along the waterfalls (where you can spot turtles sunbathing) and feel far away from Manhattan.

320 **STRAWBERRY FIELDS**

West side of the park, betw W 71st and 74th St

A mandatory stop for those looking to connect with that songwriter from Liverpool, whose life was taken in front of his home at The Dakota building, around the corner. It's touristy, but maintains a somber, peaceful and respectful tone with The Garden of Peace, and the 'Imagine' mosaic built with funds donated by Yoko Ono.

5 *great neighborhood*
WALKS

321 TRIBECA
③

Immerse yourself in NYC's oldest neighborhood. See the earliest examples of decorative cast-iron buildings: Cast Iron House, 67 Franklin St; Obsidian House, 93 Reade St; 131 Duane St. The charming Hook & Ladder 8 firehouse from *Ghostbusters* at 14 N Moore St, and the row houses, on Harrison and Washington St.

322 WILLIAMSBURG
⑨

Take a stroll along Bedford Avenue. Start south at the Williamsburg Bridge and meander your way up all the way to McCarren Park. Williamsburg is buzzing with great restaurants, trendy cafes, bars and boutiques. This neighborhood still shows some rough edges and has a lot of street art.

325 BROOKLYN BRIDGE PARK

323 UPPER WEST SIDE

⑦

The UWS is known for its pretty tree-lined streets lined with characteristic townhouses — snake up and down the blocks from 69th to 76th, from Central Park West to Columbus. The Ansonia Hotel, a castle-like behemoth takes up an entire block on Broadway between 73rd and 74th Streets. Near the Museum of Natural History, NY Historical Society, The Dakota.

324 WEST VILLAGE

④

Bedford Street from Christopher to Houston is the fastest way to walk through the Village to Soho. On the way: narrowest house 75½ Bedford St; oldest house 77 Bedford St; some think the house on the corner of Grove and Bedford Streets (17 Grove) is the oldest; 102 Bedford St was renovated by an amateur architect in an odd style.

325 BROOKLYN BRIDGE PARK / DUMBO

Carousel at the end of Old Dock St
Dumbo, Brooklyn ⑩
janescarousel.com

You can feel New York's past lingering in the streets, but also its future, thanks to the creative enterprises that have moved in. Must dos: take a picture on the corner of Water/Washington with Brooklyn Bridge looming; go for a ride on a beautifully restored 1922 carousel, housed in a glass pavilion designed by Jean Nouvel.

5 historic places in
BROOKLYN HEIGHTS

326 **WOODEN HOUSES**
Along Middagh St
Brooklyn Heights ⑩

Wooden housing was outlawed in
Brooklyn Heights in 1852 but some
original wooden houses have remained
along picturesque Middagh Street, namely
numbers 31 and 24, on the corner of
Willow Street. Truman Capote lived at
70 Willow St, by the way, and is known to
have said: "I live in Brooklyn. By choice."

327 **BROOKLYN
HISTORICAL SOCIETY**
128 Pierrepont St
(at Clinton St)
Brooklyn Heights ⑩
+1 718 222 4111
brooklynhistory.org

This museum aims to keep Brooklyn's
400-year history alive. It's housed in
a beautiful red brick Romanesque Revival
building from 1878 with arched windows
and terra cotta detailing, including
busts depicting the famous – Benjamin
Franklin, Shakespeare, Beethoven,
and Michelangelo. The interior houses
a library with elegantly carved wooden
bookcases and a dramatic mezzanine
where many parties are held.

328 CHASE BANK BUILDING

177 Montague St
(at Clinton St)
Brooklyn Heights ⑩

This Italian Renaissance style building was built between 1914 and 1916 as a bank, and remarkably is still in use as a bank today. Take in the grandeur of the hall on the ground floor, with chandeliers hanging from the coffered ceiling, and the row of teller windows. The only signs of modernity are the ATMs that look totally out of place here.

329 SUPREME COURT BUILDING APPELLATE DIVISION

45 Monroe Place
(at Pierrepont St)
Brooklyn Heights ⑩
+1 718 875 1300

This stately Classical Revival courthouse was built between 1936 and 1938, in the style that flourished in the era of the Depression. It sits on the cusp of a residential neighborhood made up of mansions. Inside you can admire a two-story courtroom with a gold-leafed coffered ceiling.

330 BROOKLYN HEIGHTS PROMENADE

Betw Remsen
and Middagh St
Brooklyn Heights ⑩
nyharborparks.org

This 1800-foot (or 0.5-kilometer) walkway is also known as the Esplanade, and runs along the western edge of Brooklyn Heights. It's famous for its views of Lower Manhattan across the East River. Near Cranberry Street take the Squibb Park Bridge which meanders over the Brooklyn-Queens Expressway and connects to pier 1 of Brooklyn Bridge Park.

5 *must-see*
SPORTS

331 BASEBALL: THE YANKEES
AT: YANKEE STADIUM
1 East 161st St
(betw River and
Jerome Ave)
The Bronx ⑧
+1 718 293 4300
mlb.com/yankees

The pin-striped Yankees are still the gold standard of NY baseball, whose players earn the big salaries, and have many championships under their belts. Watch them play in their newish 2,3-billion-dollar stadium (most expensive one ever built). They get food from some of NYC's best restaurants, like Parm, Lobel's of New York, and Brother Jimmy's BBQ.

332 US OPEN
AT: USTA BILLIE JEAN KING
NATIONAL TENNIS CENTER
ARTHUR ASHE STADIUM
Flushing Meadows
Corona Park
124-02 Roosevelt Ave
(betw 60th and 61st St)
Queens
+1 718 760 6363
usopen.org

One of NYC's most sophisticated sporting events where professional tennis meets a see-and-be-seen enclave. Plenty of celebs and VIPs head to Queens each year at the end of August to watch the best in tennis compete. The matches go on for 12 days leading up to the exciting final showdowns. Tickets on sale in mid-June.

333 BASEBALL: THE METS
AT: CITI FIELD
120-01 Roosevelt Ave
(at Main St)
Queens
+1 718 507 8499
mlb.com/mets

New York's #2 baseball team probably has its most die-hard fans. The team has recently been playing very well – better than the Yankees. Shake Shack burgers can be had here, as well as celebrity-chef David Chang's chicken sandwiches. Once a year during the Subway Series, the Yankees and Mets play each other, to much NYC fanfare.

334 FIVE BORO BIKE TOUR
bike.nyc/events/td-five-boro-bike-tour

Join over 30.000 riders hitting the streets of all five boroughs on the first Sunday in May. This 40-mile ride will take you through the center of Manhattan through Central Park, touch a corner of the Bronx, come down along the East River on both sides all the way to Staten Island. Experience the city as bike-only!

335 NYC MARATHON
tcsnycmarathon.org

Every first Sunday of November parts of New York become sectioned off for the marathon, one of the most prestigious in the world with over 50.000 runners, winding its way through all five boroughs. Cheering from sidelines happens all along the 26-mile route, with fans holding signs, playing *Eye of the Tiger*, and giving high fives to the runners.

5 ways to
SIGHTSEE
via public transport

---

336 STATEN ISLAND FERRY

Whitehall Terminal
Financial District ①
siferry.com

Instead of paying for a tour to float by the Statue of Liberty, hop on the Staten Island Ferry, whose 5-mile journey takes you through the New York harbor between the tip of Manhattan to Staten Island. The ferry operates 24/7 and is free. Staten Island side is currently being developed to house a mall and towering ferris wheel.

337 IKEA EXPRESS FERRY

Wall St – Pier 11
Financial District ①
+1 212 742 1969
nywaterway.com/
ikea.aspx

Off a slip near the South Street Seaport, catch a ferry that takes you to the Ikea dock in Red Hook, Brooklyn. The 20-minute trip offers nice views of downtown. To explore Red Hook itself, take Beard St and walk 3 blocks to Van Brunt Street's many cool restaurants, including Fort Defiance. Free on the weekends.

338 NYC FERRY

ferry.nyc

If you've got to use mass transit, traveling the waterways of NYC offers a magical way to get from here to there. Focused mostly on the East River, find destinations from the tip of the Bronx to far Rockaway Beach. Kids under 44 inches ride free with stroller parking. Bikes welcome!

339 M5 BUS DOWN FIFTH AVENUE

Upper East Side ⑦ +
Midtown ⑥
bustime.mta.info

Fifth Avenue is still NYC's main upscale thoroughfare and you can get a glimpse of its shine as you ride from 59th to 42nd street. Lined with the crème de la crème: designer stores, posh hotels, Rockefeller Center. Due to traffic, you'll be moving slowly, so you can take it all in. Even more dramatic at night especially during the holidays.

340 ROOSEVELT ISLAND TRAMWAY

East 59th St
(at 2nd Ave)
Upper East Side ⑦
+1 212 832 4555
rioc.ny.gov

Use your MTA subway card and take the aerial tramway that spans the East River and connects Manhattan with Roosevelt Island – at dramatic heights. You'll experience soaring views, and perhaps a bit of acrophobia, in the 5 minutes that it takes to career you across. When you get there, take a stroll along the river.

336 STATEN ISLAND FERRY

5 cool ways to
M I N G L E *with New Yorkers*

---

341 PLAY CHESS IN THE PARK

Match wits with those who have made this a daily sport. It's usually 5 dollars a game, played in a most speedy way. Look for guys in the SW corner of Washington Square Park (some cheating and trash talk!), the west side of Union Square Park, and Central Park's Chess and Checkers House off 65th Street.

342 DINE AT THE BAR INSTEAD OF AT A TABLE

Solo and duo diners, this is your chance to engage in conversation, and dine at those restaurants where it's nearly impossible to get a reservation. Most restaurants will allow you to set up shop at the bar, but some places encourage it, like: Cosme, Union Square Cafe, Acme, Casa Mono.

343 ANNUAL FEAST OF SAN GENNARO

Along Mulberry St
Little Italy ③
sangennaronyc.org

This 11-day event in September is something that every New Yorker has done at least once. Mulberry Street turns into a carnival of sorts with musical acts, games, and authentic Italian eats. A religious procession honors the saint rumored to have survived the flames of a fiery furnace.

344 CENTRAL PARK DANCE SKATERS ASSOCIATION

Central Park ⑦
cpdsa.org

Flock to the Bandshell in Central Park to watch free-spirited dancing/skating. There are terrifically skilled performers, some who have been coming since the 70s when this phenomenon started. Weekends April-October. Inspired? Head to Pier 2 Roller Rink in Brooklyn Bridge Park, rent skates and strut your stuff.

345 WATCH A PARADE

NYC hosts over 30 parades a year, bringing out the population to view. There are the well-known spectacles, like the Macy's Thanksgiving Parade, but dig deeper to find smaller, fun processions like the colorful Lunar New Year in Chinatown, the Easter Parade where everyone dons their finest bonnets, and the Gay Pride where anyone can march.

345 GAY PRIDE

5 ways to enjoy **N Y C**
FROM THE WATER

---

346 FREE KAYAKING FROM PIER 26
AT: THE DOWNTOWN
BOATHOUSE
Hubert St
(at the Hudson River)
Tribeca ③
downtownboathouse.org

Get up close and personal on the Hudson in 20-minute spurts. NYCDB also holds free classes that will help to perfect your paddling technique, and how not to panic if you capsize. Longer guided trips are available on a first come, first serve basis. (There are six other spots to launch from around NYC.)

347 MANHATTAN BY SAIL
AT: PIER 17
89 South St
Financial District ①
+1 212 619 6900
manhattanbysail.com

Fancy a New York wine tasting cruise, or bagels and bubbles with a view? Or do you just want to explore the world's greatest harbor from a ship while listening to jazz under a full moon? Manhattan by Sail offers you exactly that, in the form of an unforgettable sailing experience on a 1929 luxury yacht – the *Shearwater* – or on the mighty *Clipper City*, the largest tall ship in New York City.

348 INTREPID SEA, AIR & SPACE MUSEUM

AT: PIER 86
West 46th St
(at 12th Ave)
Midtown West ⑥
+1 212 245 0072
intrepidmuseum.org

Like being transported back to the 1940s. There's plenty to see on this aircraft carrier, including the Concorde, historic military aircraft, the space shuttle Enterprise and a look inside a submarine – plus exhibits in the military genre. Note, during hot weather the deck can get pretty hot, or conversely, windy and cold.

349 BATEAUX NEW YORK DINNER CRUISES

AT: PIER 61
West 23rd St
Chelsea ⑤
+1 866 817 3463
cityexperiences.com

For an upscale dining experience while riding the waves, head off the pier in Chelsea for three hours of fun. It's possible to reserve tables next to the windows so you can focus on the towering skyscrapers – this boat has a glass roof, so you can see from almost any spot. Dress up and treat yourself.

350 WALK OVER THE BROOKLYN OR WILLIAMSBURG BRIDGE

Brooklyn Bridge: From the Manhattan side enter at Centre and Chambers. From the Brooklyn side enter at Tillary and Brooklyn Bridge Boulevard or at the NE side of Cadman Plaza. Less congested is Williamsburg Bridge: From the Manhattan side pedestrians and cyclists enter at Clinton and Delancey. From Williamsburg pedestrians enter at Berry Street between 5th and 6th Streets and cyclists ride up at Washington Plaza.

The 5 best ways to get
PHYSICAL

351 WHERE TO GO FOR A RUN

Thanks to NY governor Mario Cuomo, there's a running path along the Hudson River from the tip of Manhattan to the Bronx with bathrooms and kiosks along the way. In Central Park, the full loop is about 6 miles; the 1,58-mile track along the Jacqueline Onassis Reservoir is known as the 'Stephanie and Fred Shurman Running Track' in recognition of a donation for the renovation – and is the path that Dustin Hoffman runs in the movie *Marathon Man*.

352 WEST 4TH STREET BASKETBALL COURTS

Corner of West 4th St
and 6th Avenue
Greenwich Village ④

A legendary gathering spot for exemplary players and onlookers. On this smaller than regulation-size court, also known as 'The Cage', tough physical play is the norm. It's fast and hard, with a lot of yelling and unwanted coaching from the courtside. Exhilarating to watch the talented players, some of whom become NBA stars, like Knick Anthony Mason.

353 TRAPEZE SCHOOL NEW YORK

Pier 40
Tribeca ③
+1 212 242 8769
trapezeschool.com

If you've ever dreamed of flying through the air with the greatest of ease, then here's your chance. This school will have you up and swinging in no time. Also offer stuff for kids and a variety of aerial and circus-style fun. Two locations: year-round in Williamsburg, outdoors from May – Oct by Pier 40 in Hudson River Park.

354 THE CLIFFS AT DUMBO

99 Plymouth St
Dumbo, Brooklyn ⑩
+1 347 830 7625
thecliffsclimbing.com

Underneath the Manhattan Bridge on the banks of the East River in Dumbo, this must be one of the coolest and most scenic spots to practice the ever so popular sport of bouldering. One of the largest outdoor climbing areas in the USA where climbers of all levels gather. The view is an added bonus.

355 PILATES HABITAT

192 3rd Avenue
(betw E 17th and 18th St)
Gramercy ⑤
+1 917 265 8954
pilateshabitat.com

Behind the green door a stairway leads you up to a tranquil, sky-lit workout space. It's all about innovation here, with challenging Pilates machine classes (including acro-Pilates and stretch classes), and private Gyrotonic sessions, which uses a pulley-system that stretches as you go, a favorite of dancers. Teachers here are passionate and creative in their choices of moves.

5 eras to witness N Y C
in B O O K S and M O V I E S

---

356 HISTORY AND ORIGINS OF MANHATTAN

Forever by Pete Hamill takes you through Manhattan's earliest days to the present, with an imaginative tale of a man who is graced with the ability to live forever; *Burr* by Gore Vidal paints a portrait of the early city and its political dramas; *Manahatta* by Eric Sanderson illustrates the city's wild, natural beginnings.

357 50S, 60S, 70S DYNAMICS

Just Kids, Patti Smith's memoir of her friendship with artist Robert Mapplethorpe, paints an accurate picture of Soho's artist beginnings and subculture of Manhattan; *Sleeping with Bad Boys* by Alice Denham, is an aspiring writer's tell-all of her trysts with the famous in the 1950s. Movies *Taxi Driver* and *Rosemary's Baby* capture the ultra gritty 60s and 70s city.

358 RE-LIVING THE 1980S-1990S

Desperately Seeking Susan, *American Psycho*, and *Do the Right Thing* are three films depicting NYC in the scene-changing eighties – pitching class and race and anti-establishment groups against each other. *Killing Williamsburg* by Bradley Spinelli captures the days of a 1990s gentrifying Williamsburg which is also going through an eerie suicide spree.

359 BACK TO THE 1800S

Hester Street, a movie that tells the story of a Jewish family who immigrated to the Lower East Side and how they ultimately assimilated; *Time And Again* is the classic time-travel tale by Jack Finney whose story takes place at The Dakota and on Gramercy Park – a mystery and moving love story.

360 THROUGH THE EYES OF WOODY ALLEN

Witness this artist's romance with the city. *Manhattan* is brilliant in its black-and-white cinematography, showing viewpoints and scenes from 1979. *Annie Hall*, out in 1977, highlights NYC vs LA attitudes. *Manhattan Murder Mystery* is a great slice of life focused on two couples who suspect their neighbor has murdered his wife, circa 1993.

5 things that
NEW YORKERS
just KNOW

---

361 TAXI SAVVY

No cabs in sight? The next best thing is Uber or Lyft, but to avoid costly surge pricing download the taxi apps. Arro and Curb work the same way, but with professional drivers in yellow cabs. Also good to know, when a taxi has its Off Duty sign lit, cabs can still pick you up if your destination is on their way home.

362 PUBLIC RESTROOMS

Public restrooms are few and far between. You might see some in parks, or have to stop and get something in a restaurant, but the fact is most hotel lobby's won't stop you from coming in. So act like you're staying there and take advantage. There's also NYrestroom.com that maps the city's options.

363 DRESS APPROPRIATELY

Walking is the best way to get around and really get to see all that's out there. So, bring your favorite, stylish pair of comfortable footwear that can work the scene from day to night. Smart casual outfits, athleisure, and a chill attitude can get you in almost anywhere. Black still reigns, but is waning.

364 RESTAURANT RULES

If you want to get into a hot restaurant it's best to plan ahead. Go online to *OpenTable.com*, *Resy.com*, or *exploretock.com* to check availability and reserve. Lots of restaurants are closed on Mondays, with busiest nights being Thursdays and Fridays. Summer weekends leave the city less populated, so perfect for getting that Saturday night table, especially 3-day weekends.

365 SAMPLE SALES AND POP-UPS

Find designer goods at 50-90% off. Check Chicmi.com, where they list sample sales and conveniently show others nearby – so you can really take advantage of the deals. Pop-Up stores fill empty retail space with racks of designer goods too. Go to 260samplesale.com to see who's selling. Bigger sales/shows have admission fees.

THEATER

60 WAYS
TO ENJOY CULTURE

5 well-established **GALLERIES** —————— 198

5 interesting **AVANT-GARDE GALLERIES** —— 200

5 places where you can enjoy **ART FOR FREE** —— 202

The 5 best **ART FAIRS** —————————— 204

5 must-see areas of the **MET** —————— 206

The 5 most intimate **MUSEUMS** ————— 208

5 of the best places to see **DANCE** ———— 210

5 intimate **THEATERS** ————————— 212

The 5 best places to hear **JAZZ** ————— 214

The 5 best **CLUBS** for a night out ———— 216

The 5 best places to watch **FILMS** ———— 218

5 **TV SHOWS** with a live audience ———— 220

5 well-established
GALLERIES

---

366 **DAVID ZWIRNER**
537 West 20th St
(betw 10th and
11th Ave)
Chelsea ⑤
+1 212 517 8677
davidzwirner.com

David Zwirner opened his first gallery in Soho in 1993. His latest in NYC is in a 30.000-sq-foot sleek building designed to accommodate large installations. The gallery is home to many highly regarded artists, like Jeff Koons, Yayoi Kusama, Luc Tuymans, Neo Rauch, and William Eggleston.

367 **HAUSER & WIRTH**
548 West 22nd St
(betw W 10th and
11th Ave)
Chelsea ⑤
+1 212 790 3900
hauserwirth.com

This internationally renowned and respected Swiss-owned gallery has moved its digs into temporary quarters in the former DIA space, while awaiting the construction of a brand-new space next door. The gallery represents established and emerging artists, including Mark Bradford, and Paul McCarthy and artist estates, like The Louise Bourgeois Studio.

368 GAGOSIAN GALLERY

**976 Madison Avenue
(betw E 76th and
77th St)
Upper East Side ⑦
+1 212 744 2313
*gagosian.com***

Larry Gagosian is consistently listed in the top 10 of *ArtReview*'s Power 100, with 16 galleries around the world. In New York you can visit four of them, two uptown, and two in Chelsea. If you can't afford to buy the art, you might be able to pick up something cool from the shop.

369 GLADSTONE GALLERY

**530 West 21st St
(betw 10th and
11th Ave)
Chelsea ⑤
+1 212 206 7606
*gladstonegallery.com***

American art dealer and film producer Barbara Gladstone has been a gallery owner for more than 25 years and kept her finger on the pulse. Her vision is behind some of the most successful contemporary artists today, such as Matthew Barney. The stark minimalist cube of a building includes an exhibit space with 22-foot ceilings and enormous skylight.

370 PACE GALLERY

**540 West 25th St
Chelsea ⑤
+1 212 421 3292
*pacegallery.com***

This prominent gallery represents some of the most influential international artists and estates of the 20th and 21st centuries. Catch a show by James Turrell, David Byrne, David Hockney, Jeff Koons, Alexander Calder, Willem de Kooning, Elmgreen & Dragset, or Sol LeWitt among others. What's nice is that a visit to Pace won't cost you a cent.

5 interesting
AVANT-GARDE
GALLERIES

---

371 P·P·O·W GALLERY
392 Broadway
Tribeca ③
+1 212 647 1044
ppowgallery.com

Founded in 1983 by two gutsy women with a knack for the avant-garde – Penny Pilkington and Wendy Olsoff –, P·P·O·W is still doing what it's good at, namely showcasing socially engaged work that is ahead of its time. If you want to see cool art from communities that have historically been underrepresented in the art world, P·P·O·W is the place to go.

372 BRIDGET DONAHUE GALLERY
99 Bowery, 2nd Fl.
(betw Hester and Grand St)
Lower East Side ③
+1 646 896 1386
bridgetdonahue.nyc

This is where artists go when they want to know what's happening. Thanks to Bridget Donahue's focus on underrated artists, her gallery is considered a hub of the new generation and a bright beacon on the Lower East Side. She also has a hand in the fantastic gallery Cleopatra's in Brooklyn.

373 RAMIKEN

389 Grand St
(betw Essex and
Clinton St)
Lower East Side ③
+1 917 328 4656
ramikencrucible.com

This bad-ass gallery is the brainchild of musician and artist Mike Egan, who was described by the New York Times as 'Marcel Duchamp's non-existent mischievous little brother'. He regularly hosts music performances in this raw space, whose art is the most cutting-edge, with artists like Lucas Blalock.

374 TENNIS ELBOW

AT: THE JOURNAL GALLERY
45 White St
Tribeca ③
+1 718 218 7148
thetenniselbow.org

Tennis Elbow does everything a regular gallery doesn't do. They don't represent artists; they show artists of other galleries. A new show opens every Saturday at noon, and they sell the work online through a membership-only site. Joining is free, but collectors must be approved and agree to some rules, including no resale for two years.

375 NICOLA VASSELL

138 10th Avenue
Chelsea ⑤
+1 212 463 5160
nicolavassell.com

Nicola Vassell opened her gallery after working with artists like Kehinde Wiley and advising art collectors like Swizz Beatz. It is still rare to see a contemporary art gallery owned by a Black woman in the heart of Chelsea, but this former director of both Pace and Deitch Projects shows white artists as well as artists of color in a beautiful 3500-square-foot space.

5 places where you can enjoy
ART FOR FREE

---

376 **MTA ART & DESIGN**
web.mta.info/mta/aft

As you travel through NYC's subway system, it's not just grit and grime. Founded in the 1980s, the MTA has commissioned over 300 works by emerging and established artists. Witness a wide range of murals, mosaics, poetry, music, digital art, photography. The website can help to identify your faves.

377 SOTHEBY'S

377 SOTHEBY'S

1334 York Avenue
(at E 72nd St)
Upper East Side ⑦
+1 212 606 7000
sothebys.com

So much valuable art passes through Sotheby's that it's worth the trek to the East River – you never know what you might find. Head to the auction rooms on the second floor to marvel at this month's selection of fine and decorative art, jewelry, and collectibles.

378 LOBBY PENINSULA HOTEL

700 5th Avenue
Midtown ⑥
+1 212 956 2888
peninsula.com

To celebrate their 30th anniversary, the Peninsula has curated an art installation focused on artists that made the scene in NYC during the 80s. Get a glimpse of works from Haring, Basquiat, Warhol, and more, located in the public areas of the hotel. (They also have a sweet rooftop space in case you need refreshment!)

379 MUSEUM'S FREE DAYS

ALL OVER TOWN

Check websites for exact times: TUES: Brooklyn Botanic Garden; Cooper-Hewitt; Jewish Museum. WED: Bronx Museum of the Arts; Children's Museum of the Arts. THURS: New Museum of Contemporary Art. FRI: Asia Society; MoMA; The Morgan Library; The Neue Galerie. SAT: Brooklyn Botanic Garden; Brooklyn Museum; Studio Museum in Harlem.

380 ART IN THE PARKS

MADISON SQUARE PARK
East 23rd-26th St,
betw Madison and
5th Ave
Flatiron ⑤
madisonsquarepark.org

Massive sculptures grace the lawns of Madison Square Park on an ongoing basis. Art works on view are presented by Madison Square Park Conservancy. While in the park, hit the line and enjoy a famous Shake Shack burger.

The 5 best
ART FAIRS

---

381 INDEPENDENT
VARIOUS LOCATIONS
independenthq.com

The Independent was founded in 2009 and still offers a very good mix of established and emerging commercial galleries, as well as some non-profit institutions. The first edition of this art fair took place in the former Dia Center for the Arts on West 22nd Street in Chelsea after which it moved to the slick Spring Studios in 2016. Check out the website as future editions will take place in different locations throughout the city.

382 OAF NEW YORK – OUTSIDER ART FAIR
AT: METROPOLITAN PAVILION
125 West 18th St
Chelsea ⑤
+1 212 337 3338
outsiderartfair.com

The Outsider Art Fair focuses on the work of self-taught art makers. The works on display have a naïve quality and are often produced by people who have not trained as artists or worked within the conventional structures of art production. Art dealers at this 30-year-old fair consider themselves public conversationalist more than your typical commercial art dealer.

383 THE ART SHOW

AT: PARK AVENUE ARMORY
**643 Park Avenue
(at 67th St)
Upper East Side** ⑦
+1 212 488 5550
artdealers.org

Organized by the Art Dealers Association of America (ADAA), this art show is considered to be the best one in New York, with presentations by 72 of America's leading art dealers, selling works from the 19th century to today. The show goes for five days in the beginning of March, opening with a gala preview.

384 THE ARMORY SHOW

AT: JAVITS CENTER,
MAIN ENTRANCE
CRYSTAL PALACE
**429 11th Avenue
Midtown West** ⑥
+1 212 645 6440
thearmoryshow.com

The city's premier art fair for discovering 20th- and 21st-century pieces takes place every year for 4 days in the beginning of March. There are panel discussions, artist talks, book signings, and Focus – the section to encounter new artists and galleries. From 2022 on, The Armory Show will take place in the Javits Center in Hudson Yards.

385 SPRING/BREAK ART SHOW

VARIOUS LOCATIONS
springbreakartshow.com

SPRING/BREAK is an artist-run annual exhibition in the form of an art fair. It takes place in a unique location each year, usually in underused, atypical NYC spaces. The fair offers free exhibition space to independent curators and encourages exhibitions in unusual environments. The focus is on emerging and mid-career artists, as well as installation, performance, interactive and video work.

5 must-see areas of the
MET

Metropolitan Museum of Art
1000 5th Avenue (at E 82nd St)
Central Park ⑦
+1 212 535 7710
metmuseum.org

386 PANORAMIC VIEW OF THE PALACE AND GARDENS OF VERSAILLES
Gallery 735
Inside the
American Wing

In the 1700s this was considered a form of sightseeing – rooms set up in a 360° setting which made it seem as if you were actually there. This view of Versailles by John Vanderlyn was painted in New York using the sketches that he had made at Versailles. The artist toured with his masterpiece and included a self-portrait (on the right of the Basin de Latone).

387 FRANK LLOYD WRIGHT ROOM
Gallery 745
Inside the
American Wing

The spacious living room from one of Frank Lloyd Wright's grandest prairie houses is meticulously recreated to the very last detail. The house was owned by the Little family, a member wanting a smaller house on the land chose to sell it to the Met, who have honored the original intentions of the designer, including daylight coming in through the wall of windows.

388 SHADY LADIES TOUR

Throughout the museum
shadyladiestours.com

Shady Ladies Tours points out the museum's artwork depicting courtesans, mistresses, and professional beauties throughout history – complete with their accompanying scandalous backstories, led by scholar and professor Andrew Lear, an expert on Greek and Roman erotic art. They also have a Gay Secrets of the Met and a Sexy Secrets of the Met Tours.

389 HENRY R. LUCE CENTER

Mezzanine of the American Wing

View those American fine art and decorative art objects that are not currently on display in the museum. Called 'visible art storage' this back room of the museum is open to all visitors. Meticulously arranged by material, form and chronology, the collection includes oil paintings, sculpture, furniture and woodwork, glass, ceramics, and metalwork.

390 THE ROOFTOP

This rooftop garden on top of the Met has changing art installations combined with great views of the Upper East Side and the Manhattan skyline and a small outside bar. Fatigued from discovering all the wonders at the Met, here you can have a seat, enjoy a drink/snack while overlooking the treetops of Central Park.

The 5 most intimate
MUSEUMS

---

391 **LOUIS ARMSTRONG HOUSE MUSEUM**
34–56 107th St
Queens
+1 718 478 8274
louisarmstrong house.org

This intimate historic house museum in Corona, Queens, is the house that Louis Armstrong and his wife Lucille Wilson lived in from 1943 until his death in 1971. Lucille gave ownership to New York after his passing. Since 1978, it is a National Historic Landmark that hosts concerts and educational programs.

392 **TENEMENT MUSEUM**
103 Orchard St
(at Delancey St)
Lower East Side ③
+1 877 975 3786
tenement.org

Take a guided tour and meet the residents (played by actors). This building, where more than 7000 immigrants passed through, was built in 1863. The house is staged to look exactly the way it did when the immigrants lived there. People are encouraged to share their own stories to preserve the history of NYC's early immigration.

393 NEW MUSEUM

**235 Bowery
(betw Stanton and
Rivington St)
Lower East Side ③
+1 212 219 1222**
newmuseum.org

The museum presents work of under-recognized and emerging international artists before they receive widespread attention – with works that are often considered out-of-the-ordinary. It is where gallery-owner Barbara Gladstone established the Stuart Regen Fund to support lecture series by leading international thinkers in the fields of art, architecture, design. The building itself, makes a cool statement on Bowery.

394 NEUE GALERIE

**1048 5th Avenue
(at E 86th St)
Upper East Side ⑦
+1 212 994 9493**
neuegalerie.org

The place for turn-of-the-century German and Austrian art and design. There are stunning tabletop items by Josef Hoffman and others, drawings and paintings by Gustav Klimt, Oskar Kokoschka, and Egon Schiele – all tucked inside a Beaux-Arts mansion. An authentic, lovely Viennese cafe sits inside, which also hosts live European music of the 1890s-1930s on Thursday nights.

395 DONALD JUDD HOUSE

**101 Spring St
(at Mercer St)
Soho ②
+1 212 219 2747**
juddfoundation.org

The artist purchased this building in 1968 and turned it into his playground for creating. In homage, his home and studio have been made to look exactly the way they did in 1994 – leaving everything in place (200 pieces of art and furniture plus 1800 household items). Only groups of 8 at a time can tour, book in advance.

5 of the best places to see
DANCE

---

396 JOYCE THEATER

**175 8th Avenue
(at W 19th St)
Chelsea ⑤
+1 212 242 0800
joyce.org**

The Joyce's programming covers many different styles of contemporary and cutting-edge dance like jazz-inspired tap-dancing and flamenco along with traditional ballet – and the avant-garde Ballet Hispanico. Reserve a spot at intermission to enjoy your glass of bubbly at a table and rub elbows with fellow dance enthusiasts.

397 THE KITCHEN

**512 West 19th St
(betw 10th Ave and
West St)
Chelsea ⑤
+1 212 255 5793
thekitchen.org**

For those seeking the truly outlandish and experimental. The Kitchen is one of NYC's oldest nonprofit spaces where artists like Laurie Anderson, Lucinda Childs, and Bill T. Jones have debuted. Shows feature experimental dance by innovative, boundary-pushing artists. The space also features music, theater, video, art, and talks.

398 SYMPHONY SPACE

**2537 Broadway
(at W 95th St)
Upper West Side ⑦
+1 212 864 5400**
symphonyspace.org

Symphony Space hosts music, dance, theater, film, and readings (known for Selected Shorts – where famous actors read engaging short stories). There are two performance spaces: the 800-seat Peter Jay Sharp Theatre, and the more intimate 170-seat Leonard Nimoy Thalia, named after two of their most illustrious patrons.

399 BROOKLYN ACADEMY OF MUSIC

**30 Lafayette Avenue
(betw St Felix St
and Ashland Pl)
Fort Greene,
Brooklyn ⑩
+1 718 636 4100**
bam.org

To see an eclectic mix of dance, often described as energetic, frenetic, and dazzling interpretations of classics, head to BAM. They also feature film, theater, music, and operas performed by adventurous artists, some emerging and others known masters. This venue has three theaters, the Harvey Theater, Peter Jay Sharp Building, and the Fisher Building.

400 HOUSE OF YES

**2 Wyckoff Avenue
(at Jefferson St)
Bushwick, Brooklyn**
houseofyes.org

Opened in 2016, this colorful cube pushes the boundaries of entertainment. Shows include an attractive assortment of aerialists, magicians, dancers, and live bands. If dressing up is your thing, you will fit in with this crowd, who love to arrive in outlandish and creative outfits. Doors open early, with bar and DJ while you await the show.

5 *intimate*
THEATERS

---

401 59E59 THEATERS
59 East 59th St
(betw Park and
Madison Ave)
Midtown East ⑥
+1 212 753 5959
59e59.org

A wonderful, small theater experience showcasing new work from around the world to premiere in NYC. Their four floors house three theaters running fun, innovative, and experimental works. Shows run for roughly a month, so there's always something new to see. The Brits Off Broadway series is a yearly festival that imports works from the UK.

402 LA MAMA EXPERIMENTAL THEATRE CLUB
66 East 4th St
(betw Bowery and
2nd Ave)
East Village ④
+1 212 352 3101
lamama.org

Ellen Stewart, a true supporter of the arts, founded La Mama in 1961. Since then a slew of playwrights (Sam Shepard) and celebs (Robert De Niro, Whoopi Goldberg, Bette Midler) have graced the space. Over 100 productions take place annually at their three theaters. Shows usually run for a few weeks, or can be a single performance.

403 ST. ANN'S WAREHOUSE

45 Water St
Dumbo, Brooklyn ⑲
+1 718 254 8779
stannswarehouse.org

Located in a former 19th-century tobacco warehouse, near Brooklyn Bridge Park, St. Ann's Warehouse is a state-of-the-art theater that has gained international recognition and has commissioned, produced and presented a diverse body of groundbreaking theater and concert productions connecting theater and rock 'n' roll. After four decades, it has become the artistic home of American avant-garde and international companies of stature.

404 CHERRY LANE THEATRE

38 Commerce St
(betw Bedford Ave
and Hudson St)
West Village ④
+1 212 989 2020
cherrylanetheatre.org

On one of the most quaint curving streets in the West Village is an equally becoming theater. Long a home for non-traditional and experimental works, you can sit in comfort and witness theater in an intimate setting. Productions range from new works by emerging playwrights to classics from the icons of theater.

405 THEATRE 80 ST MARKS

80 St Marks Place
(betw 1st and 2nd Ave)
East Village ④
+1 212 388 0388
theatre80.
wordpress.com

Enter through an old tavern to experience this intimate theater with history – a pioneer in the downtown arts movement. Sidewalk out front still features footprints of visiting stars – including Gloria Swanson. Today, their shows range from traditional Shakespeare to avant-garde works from new authors.

The 5 best places to hear
JAZZ

406 ZINC BAR
82 West 3rd St
(betw Thompson
and Sullivan St)
Greenwich Village ④
+1 212 477 9462
zincbar.com

A cool subterranean jazz club, with an art deco, red-velvety, Parisian vibe. It holds the spirit of the place when it was home to Thelonious Monk and Billie Holliday. Finger tap to African, Latin and Brazilian rhythms on the weekends. Thursdays feature the wild card sets.

407 SMALLS JAZZ CLUB
183 West 10th St
(betw 7th Ave S and
W 4th St)
Greenwich Village ④
+1 646 476 4346
smallslive.com

A destination spot for great jazz, the atmosphere is authentic, not slick; you'll feel like you're in an old-school New York jazz club of a bygone era. No reservations. To get a preview, become a member of SmallsLIVE to watch live streams, every show has been recorded since 2007.

408 BLUE NOTE
JAZZ CLUB
131 West 3rd St
(betw MacDougal St
and 6th Ave)
Greenwich Village ④
+1 212 475 8592
bluenote.net

The spot to see the jazz's finest musicians, just look for the building with the grand piano-shaped awning. If you go to the Monday Night Series or the Late Night Groove Series you'll witness New York's up-and-coming jazz, soul, hip-hop, R&B and funk artists as well. Be prepared to stand in line.

409 BIRDLAND JAZZ CLUB

315 West 44th St
(betw 8th and 9th Ave)
Hell's Kitchen ⑥
+1 212 581 3080
birdlandjazz.com

More of a supper club than intimate venue, this space was built for world-class jazz – with great acoustics. Tune into the sounds of legendary musicians like Oscar Peterson, Diana Krall, Dave Brubeck, Tito Puente, along with big bands, while enjoying food with Cajun-influence. They host the Umbria Jazz Festival and the Django Reinhardt Festival.

410 FINE & RARE

9 East 37th St
(betw 5th and
Madison Ave)
Midtown ⑥
+1 212 725 3866
fineandrare.nyc

Like an old-time supper club, you can do dinner in style or stand at the back and sip from their collection of rare spirits. Shows nightly with no cover. Highlight: Every Saturday night Lady Gaga's bandleader and trumpeter Brian Newman's band belts out a nostalgic sampling of jazz standards and original songs with personality and flair.

408 BLUE NOTE JAZZ CLUB

The 5 best
CLUBS *for a night out*

411 **BROOKLYN MIRAGE**
AT: AVANT GARDNER
FROM EARLY MAY
THROUGH SEPTEMBER
140 Stewart Avenue
Williamsburg,
Brooklyn ⑨
+1 347 987 3146
avant-gardner.com

The Brooklyn Mirage is a spectacular outdoor sanctuary in the center of the Avant Gardner complex, an entertainment venue that occupies an entire city block of industrial East Williamsburg. The large courtyard is a mesmerizing space, surrounded by elevated towers with views, thousands of tropical plants and captivating video projections.

412 COMEDY CELLAR

412 COMEDY CELLAR

**117 MacDougal St
(betw Minetta Lane
and W 3rd St)
Greenwich Village** ④
+1 212 254 3480
comedycellar.com

This well-known comedy club was immortalized by comedian Louis C.K. in the opening credits of his TV show *Louie* and has hosted most of comedy's luminaries – who still often drop in impromptu. *The Nasty Show* on Wednesdays and Thursdays allows comics to spew out some of their more shocking material.

413 WEBSTER HALL

**125 East 11th St
(betw 3rd and 4th Ave)
East Village** ④
+1 212 353 1600
websterhall.com

The biggest and most prestigious nightclub and performance hall in New York City. Webster Hall has been around since 1886 and has seen everything from masquerade balls in the 20s to Mick Jagger and Metallica. Five different venues inside.

414 KNITTING FACTORY

**361 Metropolitan Ave
(betw N 4th and
5th St)
Williamsburg,
Brooklyn** ⑨
+1 347 529 6696
bk.knittingfactory.com

This nightclub moved from Soho to Tribeca to Williamsburg bringing its eclectic music and entertainment program. The Main Venue where the performances take place has an open floor, and The Front Bar is where you can bide time before a show, or have a more intimate experience, like comedy on Sunday nights.

415 THE SLIPPER ROOM

**167 Orchard St
(entrance on
Stanton St)
Lower East Side** ③
slipperroom.com

If you're into burlesque, comedy, dancing, circus arts, magic, and more, head to The Slipper Room, a legendary variety theater and one of the city's more popular theater and nightlife lounges, that has been around since 1999. Over the years, acts like Lady Gaga, Leonard Cohen, the Scissor Sisters and U2 have taken to the stage there.

The 5 best places to watch
FILMS

416 **ANGELIKA FILM CENTER**
18 West Houston St
(at Mercer St)
Noho ④
+1 212 995 2570
angelikafilmcenter.com

A swanky movie experience awaits in Noho's pioneer of independent films, whose roster offers a diverse mix of independent films from all over the world. It is one of the most recognized art film houses in the US and a great place to spot famous actors at one of their premieres or on a night out.

417 **METROGRAPH**
7 Ludlow St
(betw Canal and
Hester St)
Lower East Side ③
+1 212 660 0312
metrograph.com

Revered old films and independent new ones are on the agenda of this theater that harks back to the glam of the 1920s. Events also take the stage with exclusive premieres, rare archival print screenings, and book signings. A restaurant on the premises modeled after Hollywood backlot cafeterias, is where you'll grab a bite before/after the show.

418 NITEHAWK CINEMA

**136 Metropolitan Ave
(at Berry St)
Williamsburg,
Brooklyn** ⑨
+1 718 782 8370
nitehawkcinema.com

If you'd like dining and cocktailing to be a part of your viewing experience, then this place is for you. Tiny tables with cup holders are stationed in between the rows of seats. Menus are sometimes themed to match the particular film – ranging from current releases to its free Simpsons Club on Monday nights.

419 FILM FORUM

**209 West Houston St
Greenwich Village** ④
+1 212 727 8110
filmforum.org

This nonprofit movie theater in Greenwich Village opened in 1970 and has cultivated a real community of film buffs. Film Forum screen as many as 400 or 500 films each year. Cinephiles come here to laugh, cry and argue, but also to get an education. A dedicated audience, good concessions and great programming make it one of the best movie theaters in the city.

420 MUSEUM OF THE MOVING IMAGE

**36-01 35th Avenue
(betw 36th and
37th St)
Astoria, Queens**
+1 718 777 6888
movingimage.us

Housed in a high tech, futuristic wonder is a theater with the biggest screen in NYC. Guest directors and actors often appear on the scene along with the films: new releases, themed festivals, and cinema classics. Ongoing and special exhibits, many interactive, are designed to thrill movie buffs.

5 TV SHOWS
with a live audience

---

421 THE VIEW

AT: ABC TELEVISION
STUDIOS
**57 West 66th St
(betw Columbus Ave
and Central Park W)
Upper West Side ⑦
1iota.com/show/385/
the-view**

Get an up-close-and-personal view of the
chatty daytime talk show, created by
journalist Barbara Walters over 20 years
ago. Their signature panel of women,
celebrity guests and a focus on current
events make the show a slice of history.
Tickets are free but they overbook to
assure a full audience, so get there early.

**422 WENDY WILLIAMS
SHOW**

AT: CHELSEA STUDIOS
**221 West 26th St
(betw 7th and 8th Ave)
Chelsea ⑤
+1 212 401 6600
wendyshow.com/
the-show**

This daily hour-long show with a live
studio audience is presented by the
audacious Wendy Williams. It's a campy
show all about pop-culture with a roster
of celebrity guests and interviews, in
addition to her signature segments –
Hot Topics and covering of the headlines
in entertainment. Reserve a spot online,
tickets are free.

423 TODAY SHOW

OUTSIDE NBC STUDIO 1-A
**Rockefeller Plaza
Midtown** ⑥
visit.today.com

The *TODAY* Show airs live between 7 and 10 am – you can be part of the crowd watching through the window while waving a poster. Anchors greet the crowd at 8 am, so get there at 6 if you want to be in front. See their website for details on how to meet the hosts.

424 SATURDAY NIGHT LIVE

AT: NBC STUDIO 8-H
**30 Rockefeller Plaza
Midtown** ⑥
nytix.com

This show is famous for being a political and *zeitgeist* barometer, as well as for being the cradle for future comedy talent. You cannot choose the date for your tickets, so your best bet is to try for stand-by tickets distributed at 7 am on the morning of a taping September to May. Send an email during the month of August for the upcoming season to: *snltickets@nbcunio.com*.

425 THE DAILY SHOW WITH TREVOR NOAH

AT: COMEDY CENTRAL
**733 11th Avenue
(betw W 51st
and 52nd St)
Midtown West** ⑥
+1 212 586 2477
showclix.com

Trevor Noah has taken the challenge of replacing Jon Stewart in this American news satire and late-night talk show, which airs Monday through Thursday on Comedy Central. Reserve up to 4 tickets online, and make sure to line up at noon to ensure entry, since reserving does not guarantee you will be admitted.

RINK AT BRYANT PARK

25 THINGS TO DO WITH CHILDREN

The 5 best PLAYGROUNDS —————————— 224

5 of the best spots in CENTRAL PARK for kids —— 226

5 places to ICE SKATE ————————————— 228

5 MUSEUMS children will love———————— 230

5 kid-friendly RESTO'S / BARS —————————— 232

The 5 best
PLAYGROUNDS

426 PIERREPONT PLAYGROUND

Pierrepont Place
(end of Pierrepont St)
Brooklyn Heights ⑩
nycgovparks.org

Adjacent to the Brooklyn Heights Promenade with best views of the southern tip of Manhattan's Financial District. Not as flashy as other playgrounds – old school even, but the serene location gives it a homey feel. An annual Halloween parade and Easter Egg hunt are wonderful local activities kids could indulge in.

427 PIER 51 PLAYGROUND

Along the West Side
Highway (at Jane St)
West Village ④
+1 212 627 2020
hudsonriverpark.org

This playground is situated on a pier jutting into the Hudson River right near Little Island, and is loaded with things to climb on. Showers, sprinklers, and streams of running water allow for splashing and cooling off in the summer as does the small ice-cream and drink cart. Perfect spot for runners with strollers to end up at.

428 TOMPKINS SQUARE PARK

Betw Avenue A
and East 7th St
East Village ④
nycgovparks.org

Set in the East Village and therefore slightly rougher around the edges, this park services the neighborhood with a traditional playground. There are grassy lawns too, next to basketball courts where older kids skateboard. A public pool straddles the northern stretch of the park.

429 BROOKLYN BRIDGE PARK

Along the waterfront
North and south of
Brooklyn Bridge
Brooklyn Heights ⑩
brooklynbridgepark.org

A welcome respite from the hustle and bustle, this green area sits right on the East River, Brooklyn side. Several piers make up this fun-filled park, outfitted with a giant slide, jungle gym, swings, carousel, and water features. Amazing views of downtown Manhattan. Kid-friendly entertainers abound during the summer.

430 WASHINGTON SQUARE ASTROTURF PLAYGROUND

Along MacDougal St
and Washington Sq S
Greenwich Village ④
+1 212 588 5659
*washingtonsquarepark
conservancy.org*

The southwest corner of Washington Square Park contains a glossy, bright green, fake-grass area which allows kids to get a little wild. Outfitted with a rope net ladder for climbing, it sits under tall shady trees. As kids scamper about, adults can enjoy sounds of jazz from local street musicians.

427 PIER 51 PLAYGROUND

5 of the best spots in
CENTRAL PARK
for kids

Central Park ⑦

431 HECKSCHER PLAYGROUND

7th Avenue & Central Park South Playground runs from W 61st to 63rd St
centralpark.com

Oldest and largest playground in the south end of the park, with slides, swings, and seesaws and a man-made aqueduct connected to a natural rock formation. Run up the rock, go down other side to get involved in a pick-up baseball or kickball game on the Heckscher Ballfields directly to the north.

CENTRAL PARK

432 STATUES: HANS CHRISTIAN ANDERSON AND ALICE IN WONDERLAND

West of Conservatory Water at 74th St
centralpark.com

Makes for great photo ops. Anderson is depicted reading from his book *The Ugly Duckling* with duck listening attentively. Storytelling of *The Little Mermaid* and *Thumbelina* takes place during summer on Saturday mornings rain or shine. Close by is *Alice in Wonderland*, a statue kids love to climb on.

433 THE CENTRAL PARK CAROUSEL

Southern end of park near East 65th St
+1 212 452 0707
centralparknyc.org/ locations/carousel

Open from late spring throughout the summer is an old-fashioned carousel with over 50 beautifully painted and carved wooden horses who trot along to lively calliope music. For younger children, parents are allowed to stand alongside their kids. Tickets are to be purchased with cash on-site: 3,25 dollars per ride.

434 BALTO STATUE

West of East Drive and E 67th St (north of the Zoo)
centralpark.com

For dog-loving tots, take the trek to see Balto, the Siberian husky sled dog immortalized in the book and film. Just north of the Tisch Children's Zoo, Balto sits atop a rock waiting for children to climb up. A true story – his heroic deeds saved the ailing residents of Nome, Alaska.

435 CENTRAL PARK ZOO

At East 64th St and 5th Avenue
+1 212 439 6500
centralparkzoo.com

The east side of the park is home to the zoo, where cats gracefully jump on rocks, animated penguins and puffins enjoy a feeding, and bears explore their rocky habitat. The Tisch Children's Zoo is a special section just for kids, featuring scampering goats and potbelly pigs available for hugging and petting.

5 places to
ICE SKATE

---

436 LEFRAK CENTER AT LAKESIDE
AT: PROSPECT PARK
(near the Parkside & Ocean Ave entrance)
Brooklyn ⑪
+1 718 462 0010
lakesidebrooklyn.com

For ice skating in a more natural setting, head to Brooklyn. This new 16.000-square foot ice skating rink, opens November through March, has an area open to the skies, and a section under a modern roof structure. During the summer, the same space houses a fountain and the Bluestone Café with indoor and outdoor seating around.

437 THE RINK AT ROCKEFELLER CENTER
45 Rockefeller Plaza
(5th Ave, betw 49th and 50th St)
Midtown ⑥
+1 212 332 7654
rockefellercenter.com

From the beginning of October thru April, this classic ice skating rink fills everyone with holiday cheer. Skate while being overseen by the golden statue of Prometheus, and other envious onlookers. When you're done skating, delight the kids with a visit to the best Lego store on Fifth Avenue through the Promenade.

438 THE RINK AT BRYANT PARK

(October 30 thru
1st week of March)
Betw W 40th and
42nd St and betw 5th
and 6th Ave
Midtown ⑥
+1 212 661 6640
bryantpark.org

Bryant Park, which sits behind the majestic New York Public Library, is slightly magical in summer but even more so in winter. Skate while listening to Frank Sinatra at this rink with a view: the green glass Verizon tower sits next to the Bank of America on 42nd Street and 6th Avenue. During the holidays, boutique shops set up kiosks.

439 WOLLMAN RINK

AT: CENTRAL PARK
East side of Central
Park betw E 62nd
and 63rd St
Central Park ⑦
+1 212 439 6900
wollmanskating
rink.com

Another rink with NYC skyscrapers as the backdrop. You may remember seeing it in the climactic, but thoroughly predictable, scene at the end of the movie *Serendipity*. Open late October to early April, there's a skating school open every day that caters to parents and toddlers. Pure magic.

440 THE RINK AT BROOKFIELD PLACE

230 Vesey St
Battery Park City ①
+1 917 391 8982
bfplny.com

If you want to be near the edge of the water downtown, this is the skating spot for you. Located conveniently behind the Winter Garden and near Hudson Eats and Le District food markets, this space beats Rockefeller center in terms of size. They also offer parent and child skate lessons.

5 MUSEUMS
children will love

441 CHILDREN'S MUSEUM OF THE ARTS

103 Charlton St
(betw Hudson
and Greenwich St)
Soho ③
+1 212 274 0986
cmany.org

Colorful and playful, this interactive museum for kids caters to kids ages 1 to 15 with classes that allow them to create their very own art – guided by in-house artists. Children have the space to get super creative with drawing, sculpture, sound art, and stop-motion animation. Exhibitions are designed to spark their imaginations.

442 BROOKLYN CHILDREN'S MUSEUM

145 Brooklyn Avenue
Crown Heights,
Brooklyn
+1 718 735 4400
brooklynkids.org

Housed under a bright yellow steel roof is a museum devoted to inspiring children. There are rooms which encourage play, while exhibits educate kids about culture and the natural world. The sensory room encourages exploration and was developed by a team of experts who welcome all, including those with autism. Artists interact with children.

443 NEW YORK TRANSIT MUSEUM

99 Schermerhorn St
(corner of Schermer-
horn and Court St)
Brooklyn ⑩
+1 718 694 1600
nytransitmuseum.org

Kids have a blast exploring vintage trains and buses in this museum that has taken over a defunct subway station. The specimens on site span from the late 1800s to the 1960s. Kids allowed behind the wheel! Entrance is a little tricky: look for a fake subway entrance just off Boerum Place.

444 AMERICAN MUSEUM OF NATURAL HISTORY

200 Central Park West
Upper West Side ⑦
+1 212 769 5100
amnh.org

A stellar museum for kids and their parents and one of NYC's most kid-friendly museums. From the Rose Center for Earth and Space and dinosaurs to Lucy, the most complete early hominid skeleton and the iconic blue whale in the Irma and Paul Milstein Family Hall of Ocean Life, as well as artifacts of Asian and European civilizations. It's all there!

445 CHILDREN'S MUSEUM OF MANHATTAN

212 West 83rd St
(betw Broadway
and Amsterdam Ave)
Upper West Side ⑦
+1 212 721 1223
cmom.org

Immersive exhibits are the charm of this 5-story museum. Here kids up to age 6 can learn about culture, history and science in the most fun way. There are classes and workshops geared to delight children like Gross Biology – which will have kids screaming ewwwwww, and The Music in Me! taught by TV star Laurie Berkner.

5 kid-friendly
RESTO'S / BARS

---

446 ELLEN'S STARDUST DINER

1650 Broadway
(at W 51st St)
Times Square ⑥
+1 212 956 5151
ellensstardustdiner.com

Wannabe Broadway actors who wait tables to make money are here to delight your young aspiring entertainers. The singing waitstaff belt out show tunes to encourage outrageous behavior and singalongs, so you don't have to worry about your kids disrupting. See the latest YouTube video on their website and you'll get the drill.

447 RUBIROSA RISTORANTE

235 Mulberry St
(betw Prince and Spring St)
Nolita ③
+1 212 965 0500
rubirosanyc.com

Walking into this family-owned establishment is like walking into another era. Located near Little Italy, their pizzas are in the thin-crust NYC classic category. And what kid doesn't like pizza? Also on the menu: more classic Southern Italian fare like eggplant parmigiano and handmade pastas. Reservations are advised, as this place is popular.

448 SERENDIPITY 3

225 East 60th St
(betw E 2nd
and 3rd Ave)
Upper East Side ⑦
+1 212 838 3531
serendipity3.com

An extension of the original Serendipity, made even more famous by the movie of the same name, this place boasts a menu that kids will adore. Enticing sweets like the Frrrozen hot chocolate, a sampling of sundaes and pies, along with a full menu of familiar choices include dim sum, pot pies, and meatloaf.

449 COWGIRL

519 Hudson St
(at W 10th St)
West Village ④
+1 212 633 1133
cowgirlnyc.com

Known as the Cowgirl Hall of Fame, this kitschy Southwestern spot debuted in the eighties wanting to attract and know neighborhood friends and families. Many a child's party has been hosted providing piñatas and goody bags. Get the Frito Pie, if you dare, a bastion of crunchy chips, hot chili, cheese and onions.

450 BROOKLYN FARMACY AND SODA FOUNTAIN

513 Henry St
(at Sackett St)
Carroll Gardens,
Brooklyn ⑪
+1 718 522 6260
brooklynfarmacy andsodafountain.com

A soda shop where you can experience nostalgic NYC desserts: authentic sundaes topped with homemade syrups, ice-cream cones crafted in upstate NY, signature sodas, and milkshakes made to order. The vintage pharmacy setting is as Brooklyn as Brooklyn gets, attracting a hipster crowd – with kids.

THE JANE HOTEL

25 PLACES TO SLEEP

5 *of the* HIPPEST HOTELS ———————— 236

5 MID-PRICED *and* COOL *hotels* ———————— 238

5 HIGH-END *hotels* ———————— 240

5 *hotels for a* SHOESTRING BUDGET ———— 242

5 *boutique hotels* OUTSIDE MANHATTAN —— 244

5 of the
HIPPEST HOTELS

451 11 HOWARD

11 Howard St
(at Lafayette St)
Soho ②
+1 212 235 1111
11howard.com

If you want to be near everything chic and unique. One of the newer hotels in town boasts eco-friendly hospitality expressed in a minimalist natural design, with major artwork throughout. Le Cou Cou and The Blond are the hotspots of the moment.

452 PUBLIC HOTEL

215 Chrystie St
(betw E Houston
and Stanton St)
Lower East Side ③
+1 212 735 6000
publichotels.com

For those seeking a dreamland of slick design. Rooms are modern and tech-savvy, with the most spectacular restaurants and experiences right inside. House of X, offers a spicy, theatrical experience. Wildly popular venues serve upscale cocktails and deluxe Peruvian cuisine, with a more casual pisco bar, for when you are looking for something more casual.

453 THE LUDLOW

180 Ludlow St
(betw Stanton and
Houston St)
Lower East Side ③
+1 212 432 1818
ludlowhotel.com

If you're looking for a cool place where New Yorkers like to hang out. Downtown and industrial style mark the scene in the lobby amidst plushy 70s leather furniture. By contrast, rooms are formally outfitted with drapes, antique beds, and sheepskin throws, with baths done in mosaic tile. Dinner at Dirty French is not to be missed.

454 THE BOWERY HOTEL

335 Bowery
(betw E 2nd and
3rd St)
East Village ④
+1 212 505 9100
theboweryhotel.com

For freethinkers looking to freewheel downtown. A hotel with old-world majesty expressed in faded velvet, potted palms, carved wood, layers of antique carpets and bellhops in red jackets. This is the lobby that everyone wants to get into, and makes a preference for hotel guests. Outside, the world is at your fingertips.

455 FREEHAND HOTEL

23 Lexington Ave
(at 23rd St)
Gramercy ⑤
+1 212 475 1920
freehandhotels.com/
new-york

If you're looking for a lively spot. Once a historic hotel and boarding house, this mid-priced hotel has lots to offer: three hot restaurants, a rooftop, comfy lounge area, and a nice location walking distance to the charms of Gramercy. For groups they offer a room with 2 twin bunkbeds or a queen with bunk. Lovingly restored with great architectural details.

453 THE LUDLOW

5 MID-PRICED
and COOL hotels

---

456 THE MARLTON HOTEL

5 West 8th St
(betw 5th and 6th Ave)
Greenwich Village ④
+1 212 321 0100
marltonhotel.com

For traditionalists looking to soak up true Greenwich Village spirit. A distinguished design has morphed this once flop house into something quite grand. Rooms are small, but beautifully appointed, with white marble baths outfitted with brass fixtures. The lobby is a popular NYC hangout. One block up from Washington Square Park.

457 SOHO GRAND HOTEL

310 West Broadway
(betw Canal and
Grand St)
Soho ②
+1 212 965 3000
sohogrand.com

For those who plan on hitting all the designer shops. Still trendy, who can resist the comfortable, voluptuous lounges which grace the second floor. You can totally relax in the comfy upscale rooms too, decked out in beiges and taupes, knowing that you are near to all that is Soho, but at the quieter end of the spectrum.

458 ARCHER HOTEL

45 West 38th St
(betw 5th and 6th Ave)
Midtown ⑥
+1 212 719 4100
archerhotel.com

If you're looking for views for less cash.
A sprawling 22-story hotel in an area that's close to everything, but a little off the beaten track. They have a lobby bar plus a cool rooftop bar with winning views of the Empire State Building. Rooms are small but smartly laid out, with thoughtful touches and cushy beds when you are ready to call it a night.

459 GILD HALL, A THOMPSON HOTEL

15 Gold St
(betw Platt St
and Maiden Lane)
Financial District ①
+1 212 232 7700
thompsonhotels.com

If you want to stay in the oldest part of Manhattan. Don't let the plain brick facade fool you. Inside is a jewel of a hotel sporting the tone of a gentleman's lodge – in tanned leather and polished wood. Rooms are sizable with marble baths. Close to subways for when you want to whisk uptown.

460 WALKER HOTEL

52 West 13th St
(betw 5th and 6th Ave)
Greenwich Village ④
+1 212 375 1300
walkerhotel.com

If you love the village and walking everywhere.
Gas lanterns adorn the entryway in this hotel evoking past times. The lobby is somewhat grand with velvet couches and a fireplace, and rooms are decently sized and priced, with art deco flavor. Lots to do in any direction from the front door.

5 HIGH-END
hotels

461 THE MARK

25 East 77th St
(at Madison Ave)
Upper East Side ⑦
+1 212 744 4300
themarkhotel.com

For the high-minded design connoisseur.
A hotel with an edgy, posh design by
Jacques Grange situated in Manhattan's
most elegant neighborhood. Providing
care and services beyond the 5-star
standard, private local phone numbers
can be assigned, or a car with driver, and
lucky kids can be treated to indoor tents
and cookies from The Mark, Jean-Georges
Vongerichten's restaurant.

462 THE PIERRE

2 East 61st St
(at 5th Ave)
Upper East Side ⑦
+1 212 838 8000
thepierreny.com

If you're looking for timeless, old-world luxury.
Featured in many films, history and
beauty is what you'll find here. See the
newly restored murals in The Rotunda
(find Jackie O.). Off the lobby is the Two
E Bar, one of the classiest, undiscovered
rooms in NYC great to meet up for
a cocktail, snack, or afternoon tea.
Rooms are sedately decked out.

463 NOMO

9 Crosby St
(betw Howard
and Grand St)
Soho ②
+1 646 218 6400
nomosoho.com

If you love a fantasy and shopping. Inspired by Jean Cocteau's *La Belle et la Bête*, this hotel lures you in through a dramatic courtyard of ivy-clad, metal framework. Its glass-roof restaurant is highlighted by sunlight flooding its groupings of chandeliers. Special services include personalized shopping experiences and in-room custom suit design.

464 THE WILLIAM VALE

111 North 12th St
(betw Wythe Ave
and Berry St)
Williamsburg,
Brooklyn ⑨
+1 718 631 8400
thewilliamvale.com

If you want to do Williamsburg in style. A spectacular, futuristic design by Albo Liberis perches dramatically above Brooklyn. Every single room features work of local artists, and has a balcony with unobstructed views. The rooftop bar is the new hot spot, capitalizing on its height with viewing scopes stationed around the space for an even closer look.

465 CROSBY STREET HOTEL

79 Crosby St
(betw Prince and
Spring St)
Soho ②
+1 212 226 6400
firmdalehotels.com

If you are looking for homey elegance. The scale and peacefulness of this eco-conscious hotel is immediately felt upon entering. Newly built, each room is uniquely styled by London designer Kit Kemp and has industrial oversized windows to bring in the light. Crosby Bar is a popular NY meeting spot for cocktails and afternoon tea.

5 hotels for a
SHOESTRING BUDGET

466 **POD 39**

145 East 39th St
(betw 3rd and
Lexington Ave)
Murray Hill ⑥
+1 212 865 5700
thepodhotel.com

For those whose only desire is to be out and about. Streamlined, compact rooms offer just what you need to stay in NYC and have extra cash to run around with. Bonuses: a whimsical rooftop space, with tacos, and a colorful lobby with room to relax or play a game of ping-pong and meet fellow travelers.

468 THE JANE HOTEL

467 THE GATSBY HOTEL

135 East Houston St
(at Forsythe St)
Lower East Side ③
+1 212 358 8844
gatsbyhotelnyc.com

If you are looking to hit all the bars on the Lower East Side. An unassuming brick building with simple and tastefully sparse rooms sits on the border of the LES, East Village, and Nolita neighborhoods. Staff is friendly and accommodating.

468 THE JANE HOTEL

113 Jane St
(betw Washington
and West St)
Meatpacking
District ④
+1 212 924 6700
thejanenyc.com

If you're just looking for a room to crash in a happening hotel. Teeny tiny rooms, most without a private bath, with Victorian styling, that once housed survivors from the Titanic. The good news is that you'll be IN at the grandiose, lively bar downstairs, and are situated in a most fantastic part of town.

469 COLONIAL HOUSE INN

318 West 22nd St
(betw 8th and 9th Ave)
Chelsea ⑤
+1 212 243 9669
colonialhouseinn.com

For those who prefer an intimate setting. A bed-and-breakfast with a decidedly gay clientele, but open to all. Half the 20 rooms have private baths. Suites are available and sleep up to 5 guests, one facing a private garden and the other with kitchenette. Founded by Mel Cheren, known as 'The Godfather of Disco'. ·

470 PARK SOUTH HOTEL

124 East 28th St
(betw Park and
Lexington Ave)
Nomad ⑤
+1 212 448 0888
jdvhotels.com

For the person who loves to walk. This location offers quick strolls to many city icons: only 11 minutes to the Empire State Building, Flatiron Building, and Gramercy. Two restaurants plus the seasonal happening rooftop provide on-site eats. Rooms are smartly decorated and equipped. Those who love Indian food will find a mecca only steps away.

5 boutique hotels
OUTSIDE MANHATTAN

471 **MCCARREN HOTEL & POOL**

160 North 12th St
(betw Bedford Ave
and Berry St)
Williamsburg,
Brooklyn ⑨
+1 718 218 1060
mccarrenhotel.com

For those with bathing suit bods. This hotel's rooms look down upon one of New York's largest swimming pools. It carries a minimalist, yet happy design, with pops of color throughout, especially in its rooftop bar providing views and craft cocktails.

472 **THE BROOKLYN – A HOTEL**

1199 Atlantic Avenue
Bedford-Stuyvesant,
Brooklyn ⑪
+1 718 789 1500
thebrooklynny.com

If you're planning on exploring Brooklyn for less. Located in the rapidly gentrifying, though still gritty, Bed-Stuy neighborhood, about a half hour subway ride from Manhattan. Guestrooms are spacious, laid out railroad style with one room leading to the next, with nostalgic murals of Brooklyn architectural icons. Slick bathrooms. No room service, but breakfast buffet in the lobby.

473 **BORO HOTEL**

38-28 27th St
(betw 38th and
39th Ave)
Long Island City
+1 718 433 1375
borohotel.com

If you want to be near the ethnic eats of Astoria. Across from the Upper East Side of Manhattan is yet another area getting a modern makeover. This new hotel's got the views – plus the nice price. Rooms feature a wall of windows, balconies, against a backdrop of raw cinderblocks and white oak floors. Rooftop, of course.

474 **THE WILLIAMSBURG HOTEL**

96 Wythe Avenue
(at N 10th St)
Williamsburg,
Brooklyn ⑨
+1 718 362 8100
thewilliamsburg
hotel.com

For those on the cutting edge. An austere slim exterior belies the stylish delights within. Beckoning, rich-turquoise tiled baths with brass fixtures, a mix of tufted natural leather and cool, reclaimed-wood parquet floors add to the homey digs. There's a swimming pool on the roof and a bar disguised as a water tower.

475 **NU HOTEL**

85 Smith St
(betw Atlantic Ave
and State St)
Brooklyn Heights ⑩
+1 718 852 8585
nuhotelbrooklyn.com

For the movers and shakers. Experience clean lines with touches of glamour, in one of Downtown Brooklyn's original boutique hotels. Playful touches like hammocks and colorful murals painted by street artists make each room different and interesting. Only snacks available in the hotel, but close to many celebrated Brooklyn eateries. Check out their packages/deals.

CONEY ISLAND

25 ACTIVITIES FOR WEEKENDS

The 5 best **DAY TRIP** destinations ———————— 248

The 5 cosiest ways to spend a weekend
in the **CATSKILLS** ———————————— 250

5 scenic places for **ANTIQUEING+** ————— 253

5 great escapes in the **OTHER BOROUGHS** —— 255

5 **LONG ISLAND** treasures ———————— 258

The 5 best
DAY TRIP
destinations

**476 SANDY HOOK
BEACH FERRY**
3 LOCATIONS IN MANHATTAN
+1 800 262 8743
seastreak.com

Enjoy a cocktail on the roof as you speed through the harbor, then shuttle to the beach – in 40 minutes flat. There's a family-friendly beach, as well as a clothing-optional stretch at the end, where gay men go to flaunt. Bring your own lunch, or cash for the food trucks. Leave early, beaches fill up quickly.

477 STORM KING
1 Museum Road
New Windsor
+1 845 534 3115
stormking.org

An hour north of Manhattan is one of the largest contemporary outdoor sculpture gardens in America. Explore their 500 acres (200 ha) on foot, with one of their bikes, or by tour-guided tram and view their oversized pieces set into natural landscapes – open fields and woods. Open April to December, check calendar for days.

478 DIA:BEACON

3 Beekman St
Beacon, NY
+1 845 440 0100
diaart.org

Near the train station is a museum housing art on a massive scale. Spaces are dedicated to major conceptual artists of the 60s. Oversized rooms act as part of the viewing experience. After, head to Beacon Flea Market for handcrafted merch, and Denning's Point Distillery for tastings and music.

479 NORTH FORK WINE TOURS

714 Main St
Greenport, NY
Long Island
+1 631 723 0505
northforkwinetours.com

Enjoy the quieter tip of Long Island – over 40 wineries sit amongst the vineyards for a pastoral escape. Packages include round trip transportation, tastings at 3 vineyards/breweries. A picnic lunch is available, or dine at a winery while listening to live music and learning first-hand what Long Island wines are all about.

480 GOVERNORS ISLAND

New York Harbor
govisland.com

From May to October, an island right in Manhattan's harbor can feel a million miles away. A perfect spot for a picnic, bike ride, or just strolling around and admiring the view. They also host events, like their annual art fairs, storytelling and poetry festivals, so check the calendar. Ferries leave from Manhattan and Brooklyn.

The 5 cosiest ways
to spend a weekend in the
CATSKILLS

---

481 HIKING

*catskillmountaineer.com/
hiking.html*

Your guide for maneuvering through the wilderness – on foot. This site gives you topographical maps of hiking areas throughout the Catskills, marking out mileage and trek times, difficulty ratings, and descriptions of terrain. Structures are highlighted, and are paired with photos of the trails. GPS coordinates get you started. Now all you need is a nice picnic lunch.

THE CATSKILLS

482 SPRUCETON INN

2080 Spruceton Road
West Kill, NY
+1 518 989 6404
sprucetoninn.com

You can almost smell the crisp air viewing the photos on the website. Tucked in the hills of West Kill, is this B&B – standing for Bed and Bar – with super sparse, rustic rooms. Grounds offer fire pits, and no light pollution, so night skies are filled with stars. Kitchenettes and BBQs allow you to whip up something from local farms.

482 SPRUCETON INN

483 WEST KILL BREWING

2191 Spruceton Road
West Kill, NY
+1 518 989 6462
westkillbrewing.com

In the middle of pristine nowhere, you'll find beer made with locally grown and foraged ingredients the same way early settlers in the area did. Sample fruity beers made with sour cherries, elderberries, lingonberries and apples – or some uncommon flavors from local mushrooms and spruce tips. This 127-acre family farm is situated along the road with the best hiking trails.

484 BRUSHLAND EATING HOUSE

1927 County
Highway 6
Bovina Center, NY
+1 607 832 4861
brushlandeating
house.com

An inn, restaurant, and shop modeling itself on colonial times when 'eating houses' were the only socializing hub. On this single street town, the restaurant offers a simple, elegant menu run by a trio of Brooklyn ex-pats. Try one of their seasonal toasts. Stay in one of their airy rooms filled with rustic wooden furniture and accessories.

485 THE BEAR CAFÉ

295 Tinker St
(Route 212)
Woodstock, NY
+1 845 679 5555
bearcafe.com

In a former haunt of rock and roll bands, childhood friends reunited to create an upscale dining experience perched idyllically on a stream. A four-sided bar dominates the space clad in wood-paneling with hand-hewn wooden beams and a lovely fireplace. The restaurant sits next to the Bearsville Theater, where you can still hear big acts and local bands play.

5 scenic places for
ANTIQUEING +

486 LAMBERTVILLE HOUSE

32 Bridge St
Lambertville, NJ
+1 609 397 0200
lambertvillehouse.com

Historically enchanting, Lambertville was founded in 1705 and retains much of the architecture from its past. Great for shopping – they're known for their antique stores – strolling along the river, and enjoying their foodie nooks, like Lambertville House, also a hotel. For kids, the Howell Living History Farm lets them see what farm life was like in the early 1900s. New Hope, a town across the river, is more commercial.

487 VILLAGE OF COLD SPRING

85 Main St
Cold Spring, NY
+1 845 265 3611
coldspringny.gov

Take the train up the scenic Hudson Line to a charming river town. Main Street heads up from the station and is lined on both sides with affordable vintage shops, galleries, and restaurants. Hike up Little Stony Point for views of the river or through the trails at West Point Foundry Preserve, an outdoor museum.

488 THE TIME NYACK

400 High Avenue
Nyack, NY
+1 845 675 8700
thetimehotels.com/nyack

Along the Hudson, NJ side, is a quaint town known for its shopping and restaurants. The Time, its new boutique hotel, is perched at the top of town. Hike in Hook Mountain. Across the Hudson, explore Kykuit, a Rockefeller estate, the Lyndhurst Mansion, and dine at famous Blue Hill at Stone Barns restaurant.

489 HYDE PARK MANSION HOPPING

4097 Albany Post Rd
Hyde Park, NY
+1 845 229 9115
www.nps.gov/vama

Compare and contrast two mansions in a day! Vanderbilt's, and the home of Franklin Delano Roosevelt. In town, cool Main Street awaits, and a quick drive brings you to the revered Culinary Institute of America. B&B's are scattered about as well as some decent inexpensive chain hotels. Nearby Poughkeepsie offers the scenic walkway over the Hudson.

490 TOUR OF HUDSON, NEW YORK

A 2.5-hour drive brings you to Hudson, a town of historic buildings, antique stores, and the spot where Manhattan VIPs have weekend houses. We love: 26 Warren B&B and Rivertown Lodge, The Spotty Dog Books & Ale, Ca'Mea, Moto Coffee Machine. For art: Olana State Historic Site. You can also get there via Amtrak.

5 great escapes in the
OTHER BOROUGHS

---

491 WAVE HILL

West 249th St
(at Independence Ave)
Riverdale, The Bronx
+1 718 549 3200
wavehill.org

Situated high above the Hudson is a 28-acre park whose panoramas have not changed since 1843. Stroll through its many gardens and greenhouse. A mansion on the grounds features art exhibits and a cafe. Download self-guided tours. Take the train from Grand Central to Riverdale, or the 1 subway line to the end – then free Wave Hill shuttle.

492 CITY ISLAND

On the Long
Island Sound
The Bronx
cityisland.com

A quaint island lined with Victorian homes, Italian restaurants specializing in fresh seafood, and a marina. Jack's Bait & Tackle offers 4-person fiberglass boats, The New York Sailing Center has sailing classes. Less than 1,5 hour away. 6 train to Pelham Bay Park. Transfer to the BX 29 bus towards City Island.

493 FOODIE TOUR BRONX

Arthur Avenue
Belmont, The Bronx
*arthuravenue
bronx.com*

Italian movies come to life in this neighborhood that defies modernization. Experience a true Italian-American foodie haven: fresh pasta, meats, bread, cheese, and pastry shops line the street. Restaurants are crowded from the second they open, so waiting for a table is part of the fun as you mingle with the locals. A short drive from Botanical Gardens.

494 FORAGE TOURS

+1 914 835 2153
wildmanstevebrill.com

Local character Steve Brill leads nature walks which teach you to identify edible plants. Learn to distinguish something edible from something deadly in The Bronx, Brooklyn, Queens, Westchester, and Putnam counties. Steve Brill leads tours on a regular basis, with a suggested donation of 20 dollars. Check the extensive schedule and sign up for an interesting experience.

495 CONEY ISLAND

Corbin Place
to West 37 St
Coney Island,
Brooklyn
+1 718 946 1353
coneyisland.com

Coney Island offers its kitschy attractions, plus beach volleyball, a playground and an amusement park with history – and the beach, where basically anything goes. Hit Nathan's hot dog emporium. Take a spin on the antique roller coasters and ferris wheel. Witness daily feedings at the NY Aquarium. See the schedule of summer concerts and the famous Mermaid Parade.

5 LONG ISLAND

treasures

---

496 POLLOCK-KRASNER HOUSE AND STUDY CENTER

830 Springs-
Fireplace Road
East Hampton, NY
+1 631 324 4929
*stonybrook.edu/
pkhouse*

Tour the house where artists Jackson Pollock and his wife Lee Krasner drank, fought, and made art. Original floorboards with paint of Pollock's most famous poured paintings can be viewed, along with the couple's furnishings, as well as exhibits with a special focus on local artists' work. Open from May to October. Check the calendar for who's speaking at the lecture series.

497 OCEAN BEACH

Fire Island
+1 631 687 4750
www.nps.gov/fiis

On this car-free island, composed of private homes and natural parks, is Ocean Beach – one of the few areas with restaurants, bars, and boutiques along the sandy shore. Nighttime is for dancing and partying. No food or drinks allowed on the beach, though. Taste of Fire Island – discounted dinner specials – happen midweek. LIRR from Penn station, then a ferry, 2,5 hours.

498 SAGG MAIN BEACH

315 Sagg Main St
Sagaponack, NY
+1 631 728 8585

This is one of those off-the-beaten-path, local beaches – if that's possible in the Hamptons – where the share-house occupants go for sun and fun. Open to the public, but you'll need a parking permit – a 25-dollar daily pass is required for non-residents, plus one for 4x4 access. Parking is ample. Catch the super-chill drum circles which gather on Monday nights and dance on the sand.

499 TOPPING ROSE HOUSE

One Bridgehampton /
Sag Harbor Turnpike
Bridgehampton, NY
+1 631 537 0870
toppingrosehouse.com

This 1000+-dollar hotel has winter pricing at 295 dollars a night. The most charming 1842 Greek Revival mansion has a hidden spa and sleek modern design. Loaner bikes available, as well as loaner Lexuses, plus shuttle rides and free passes to the beach. There's also a farm-to-table restaurant helmed by a chef you may have heard of: Jean-Georges Vongerichten.

500 SHELTER ISLAND

Mashomack Preserve
Long Island, NY
+1 631 749 1001
shelterislandtown.us

Acquired by The Nature Conservancy in the 1980s, roughly one-third of Shelter Island is dedicated to protecting rare plant species and birds – especially breeding ospreys. To maintain the habitat, they strictly enforce a 'no pets or food' as you hike through the winding pathways. Book a tour. Get there via Uber/Lyft from the North Haven/South Ferry.

INDEX

1 Hotel Brooklyn
  Bridge 155
11 Howard 236
192 Books 120
4 Charles Prime Rib 48
5 o'Clock Somewhere
  Bar 111
56 Leonard 153
59E59 Theaters 212
63 Clinton 78
9th St. Vintage 132
ABC Kitchen 74
ABCV 72
Aedes Perfumery 141
African Burial Ground
  Memorial 165
Air's Champagne
  Parlor 101
Aldo Sohm Wine Bar 101
Allure Store 141
American Cut 42
American Museum
  of Natural History 231
Ample Hills Creamery 66
Analogue 105
Angel Orensanz
  Foundation 148
Angelika Film Center 218
an.mé /ahn-may/ 145
Archer Hotel 239
Ardesia Wine Bar 111
Argosy Book Store 116
Art in the Parks 203
Artbook @ MoMA PS1 120
Artists & Fleas 121
Attaboy 105
Bagel Hole 43
Balto Statue 227
Bar Hugo 98

Bateaux New York
  Dinner Cruises 189
Belvedere Castle 154
Bemelmans Bar 98
Bergdorf Goodman 122
Billionaire Boys Club 128
Birdland Jazz Club 215
Bite Beauty Lip Lab 140
Black Seed Bagels 44
Bleecker Street Pizza 56
Blind Tiger 95
Blossom 73
Blue Note Jazz Club 214
Bluestone Lane 84
Bohemian 61
Bonsignour 107
Boro Hotel 245
Bottino 71
Breads Bakery 29
Bridget Donahue
  Gallery 200
Brodo 62
Brooklyn Academy
  of Music 211
Brooklyn Bowl 108
Brooklyn Bridge Park 225
Brooklyn Children's
  Museum 230
Brooklyn Diner 37
Brooklyn Farmacy
  and Soda Fountain 233
Brooklyn Heights
  Promenade 181
Brooklyn Historical
  Society 180
Brooklyn Mirage 216
Brooklyn Public Library 168
Brooklyn Winery
  Wine Bar 101

Brushland Eating
  House 252
Bubby's 31
Burger Joint 49
BXL Café 107
Cadence 72
Caffe Reggio 93
Café Habana 63
Cathedral Church of
  St John the Divine 157
Caveat 90
Central Park 175, 176
Central Park Zoo 227
Chase Bank building 181
Chelsea Market 53
Cherry Lane Theatre 213
ChikaLicious
  Dessert Bar 66
Children's Museum
  of Manhattan 231
Children's Museum
  of the Arts 230
Chop-Shop 61
Chrysler Building 150
Church of the
  Transfiguration 157
City Island 255
Cloak & Dagger 121
Clover Club 87
C.O Bigelow Chemists 136
Cobblestones 132
Colonial House Inn 243
Comedy Cellar 217
Coney Island 257
Conservatory Garden 175
Cookshop 70
Covenhoven 94
Cowgirl 233
Creel & Gow 134

Crif Dogs	33	
Crosby Street Hotel	241	
Cull & Pistol	59	
Culture Espresso	85	
Cure Thrift	135	
Dashwood Books	119	
Dave's New York	126	
David Zwirner	198	
Dear Irving on Hudson	86	
DeKalb Market Hall	53	
Delmonico's	41	
Di Palo's Fine Foods	39	
Dia:Beacon	249	
Diner	45	
Dirt Candy	73	
Divya's Kitchen	73	
Domino Park	172	
Donald Judd House	209	
Dorado Tacos	63	
Dover Street Market	131	
Dyckman Farmhouse Museum	167	
Dépanneur	39	
East Village Hats	143	
East Village Meat Market / J. Baczynsky	39	
Economy Candy	136	
Eldridge Street Synagogue	156	
Ellen's Stardust Diner	232	
Elsie Rooftop	87	
Emilio's Ballato	55	
Emmy Squared	57	
Ergot Records	145	
Estela	64	
Exit9 Gift Emporium	139	
Fabulous Fanny's	142	
Fanelli Cafe	96	
Fig.19	101	
FILM FORUM	219	
Filson	125	
Fine & Dandy	124	
Fine & Rare	215	
Fishs Eddy	138	
Fivestory	129	
Flatiron Building	151	
Flex Mussels	77	
Flight Club	143	
Fonda	70	
Foodie Tour Bronx	257	
Forage Tours	257	
Franklin D. Roosevelt Four Freedoms Park	164	
Fraunces Tavern	149	
Freehand Hotel	237	
Freemans	46	
Fueguia 1833	140	
Gabriel Kreuther	79	
Gagosian Gallery	199	
Gallow Green	99	
Gem	65	
Gild Hall, a Thompson Hotel	239	
Gladstone Gallery	199	
Glass House Tavern	51	
Gnocco	55	
Governors Island	249	
Gracie Mansion	166	
Grand Central Station	149	
Grant's Tomb	165	
Greenlight	118	
Green-wood Cemetery	174	
Hamlet's Vintage	133	
Hauser & Wirth	198	
Heckscher Playground	226	
Hi-Collar	93	
Holiday Cocktail Lounge	104	
Home Sweet Home	103	
House of Yes	211	
Hurley's Saloon	111	
Hyde Park Mansion Hopping	254	
Hütte	37	
IKEA Express Ferry	184	
Independent	204	
Intrepid Sea, Air & Space Museum	189	
Inwood Hill Park	174	
Irish Hunger Memorial	164	
Jack's Wife Freda	28	
Jeffrey's Grocery	58	
JJ Hat Center	142	
Joe Coffee	84	
John Derian Company	135	
John's of 12th Street	34	
Joyce Theater	210	
Juliana's	56	
Katana Kitten	105	
Katz's Delicatessen	34	
Keens Steakhouse	41	
KGB Bar	91	
Kiehl's Since 1851	141	
King	64	
Kith	127	
Knitting Factory	217	
Kyma	77	
La Colombe Coffee Roasters	85	
La Compagnie des Vins Surnaturels	100	
La Esquina	63	
La Grenouille	36	
La MaMa Experimental Theatre Club	212	
La Pecora Bianca	32	
Lady Mendl's	88	
Lafayette Grand Café & Bakery	28	
Lambertville House	253	
Lazy Point	58	
Le Boudoir	87	
Le Charlot	69	
Le Coucou	38	
Le District	52	
Le Parisien Bistrot	69	
LeFrak Center at Lakeside	228	
Legends	107	
Library of Bronx Community College	149	
Lilia	55	
Little Island	174	
Lobby Peninsula Hotel	203	
Louis Armstrong House Museum	208	
Love Adorned	124	
Lure Fishbar	76	

Mad Hatters
(Gin &) Tea Party 89
Maman 92
MANHATTA 33
Manhattan by Sail 188
Marie's Crisis Café 109
Marshall Stack 103
Martiny's 104
Maryam Nassir Zadeh 129
Mast Books 119
McCarren Hotel
& Pool 244
Mercer Street Books 118
Mermaid Oyster Bar 59
Metrograph 218
Metropolitan Museum
of Art 206, 207
Minetta Tavern 68
Miss Lily's 46
Mokyo 65
Molly's 38
MoMA Design Store 139
Mood Fabrics 137
Morris-Jumel
Mansion 166
Morso 54
Mott Street Eatery 52
Mr. Throwback 127
MTA Art & Design 202
Murray's Bagels 43
Murray's Cheese 40
Museum of Jewish
Heritage 165
Museum of the
Moving Image 219
Museum's Free Days 203
Mustang Harry's 107
Neue Galerie 209
New Museum 209
New York by Gehry 152
New York Public Library
168
New York Transit
Museum 231
New York Vintage 133
Niche Niche 78

Nicola Vassell 201
NiLu Gift Shop 139
Nitehawk Cinema 219
No Relation Vintage 122
No.6 121
NOMO 241
North Fork
Wine Tours 249
NU Hotel 245
NYC Ferry 184
NYC Trivia League 90
OAF New York –
Outsider Art Fair 204
Ocean Beach 258
Old Homestead 41
Old Town Bar 96
Olde Good Things 135
One World Trade
Center 154
One57 153
Only NY 128
Ophelia Lounge 74
Pace Gallery 199
Park South Hotel 243
Patricia Field
ArtFashion Gallery 124
Paulie Gee's 57
Pembroke Room 89
Pete's Tavern 97
Pier 51 Playground 224
Pierrepont
Playground 224
Pietro's 36
Pink Olive 138
P.J. Clarke's 97
Pod 39 242
Pollock-Krasner House
and Study Center 258
Popbar 67
Portale 75
Prince Tea House 88
Printed Matter 144
Property 134
Public Hotel 236
P·P·O·W Gallery 200
Ramiken 201

Red Farm 60
Reformation 126
Ring Ding Bar 67
Riverside Church 156
Roberta's 57
Rockefeller Center 151
Roosevelt Island
Tramway 185
Rose Main
Reading Room 168
Rosemary's 30
Rubirosa Ristorante 232
Sagg Main Beach 259
Sandy Hook
Beach Ferry 248
Saturdays NYC 144
Schott NYC 125
Search & Destroy 126
Sen Sakana 51
Serendipity 3 233
Shake Shack 48
Shelter Island 259
Shukette 71
Shuko 65
Sid Gold's
Request Room 108
Smalls Jazz Club 214
Smithfield Hall NYC 106
Sneak Ez 128
Soho Grand Hotel 238
Sons of Essex 45
Sotheby's 203
Spark Pretty 145
Spot Dessert Bar 67
SPRING/BREAK
Art Show 205
Spruceton Inn 251
St. Ann's Warehouse 213
St Mark's Church-
in-the-Bowery 157
Staten Island Ferry 184
Storm King 248
Strawberry Fields 176
Strip House 42
Stumptown 93
Subject 102

Sullivan Street Bakery 29
SUMMIT One
   Vanderbilt 155
Suprema Provisions 54
Supreme Court
   Building 181
Sweet Polly 86
Symphony Space 211
T.A. 131
Tacombi 76
Tannen's Magic Shop 137
Tanner Smiths 110
Tarallucci e Vino 84
Tea & Sympathy 38
Temple Court 98
Tenement Museum 208
Tennis Elbow 201
Terroir Tribeca 58
The Armory Show 205
The Art Show 205
The Back Room 102
The BAR 99
The Bear Café 252
The Blue Dog 51
The Bowery Hotel 237
The Brooklyn –
   A Hotel 244
The Butcher's Daughter 29
The Campbell 75
The Cast 123
The Catskills 250, 251, 252
The Central Park
   Carousel 227
The Dead Poet 91
The Dutch 68
The Ear Inn 91
The Explorers Club 171
The Fulton 76
The Gatsby Hotel 243
The General Society
   of Mechanics and
   Tradesmen Library 171
The Great Frog 143
The High Line 172
The Jane Hotel 243
The Kitchen 210

The Lambs Club 50
The Ludlow 236
The Mark 240
The Marlton Hotel 238
The Meatball Shop 32
The Modern 79
The Morgan Library
   & Museum 167
The Musket Room 79
The New York Society
   Library 171
The Odeon 68
The Pierre 240
The RealReal 131
The Rink at
   Brookfield Place 229
The Rink at
   Bryant Park 229
The Rink at
   Rockefeller Center 228
The Rum House 110
The Slipper Room 217
The Smile 31
The Spaniard 48
The Stonewall Inn 109
The Strand 116
The Time Nyack 254
The Uncommons 108
THE WELL 93
The Whitby Bar 89
The William Vale 241
The Williamsburg
   Hotel 245
The Wren 46
Theatre 80 St Marks 213
Theodore Roosevelt
   Birthplace 167
Three Lives
   & Company 118
Tim Ho Wan USA 60
Tompkins Square
   Bagels 43
Tompkins Square
   Park 224
Top Hops Beer Shop 95
Top of the Rock 154

Topping Rose House 259
Torch & Crown 94
Tour of Hudson,
   New York 254
Town Shop Lingerie 137
Trash and Vaudeville 123
Trinity Church 149
Tía Pol 71
Tørst 95
Upland 31
Urbanspace
   Vanderbilt 52
Ursus 120
Valerie 50
Veselka 32
Via 57 west 152
Via Carota 49
Village of Cold Spring 253
Walker Hotel 239
Walker's 96
Washington
   Square Astroturf
   playground 225
Walks 177, 179
Wave Hill 255
Webster Hall 217
Welcome to the
   Johnson's 103
West Kill Brewing 252
What Goes Around
   Comes Around 133
'Wichcraft 63
Wicked Jane 75
Williamsburgh Savings
   Bank Tower 151
Wollman Rink 229
Woolworth Building 150
World Trade Center
   Oculus 152
Yama 61
Yuca Bar 31
Zabar's 40
Zinc Bar 214
Zucker's Bagels &
   Smoked Fish 44
Zum Stammtisch 34

COLOPHON

EDITING and COMPOSING — Ellen Swandiak and Katelijne De Backer

GRAPHIC DESIGN — Joke Gossé and doublebill.design

PHOTOGRAPHY — Erinn Springer — Anneliese Kristedja

ADDITIONAL PHOTOGRAPHY — Aliza Fox — p. 30, 59, 77, 100, 117, 130, 173: Paulina Kajankova — p. 170, 196: Gabriel Flores — p. 250, 251: Casey Scieszka

COVER IMAGE — Coney Island (secret 495) — Erinn Springer

The addresses in this book have been selected after thorough independent research by the authors, in collaboration with Luster Publishing. The selection is solely based on personal evaluation of the business by the authors. Nothing in this book was published in exchange for payment or benefits of any kind.

D/2022/12.005/15
ISBN 978 94 6058 3100
NUR 513, 510

© 2017 Luster Publishing, Antwerp
Fourth edition, June 2022 – Sixth reprint, June 2022
lusterpublishing.com – THE500HIDDENSECRETS.COM
info@lusterpublishing.com

Printed in Italy by Printer Trento.